Study Guide

for

Samaha's

Criminal Law

Eighth Edition

Study Guide

for

Samaha's

Criminal Law

Eighth Edition

Raymond G. Kessler
Sul Ross State University

THOMSON
WADSWORTH
Australia • Canada • Mexico • Singapore • Spain • United Kingdom • United States

Printed in the United States of America
1 2 3 4 5 6 7 07 06 05 04

Printer: Thomson West

0-534-62995-4

For more information about our products, contact us at:
Thomson Learning Academic Resource Center
1-800-423-0563

For permission to use material from this text or product, submit a request online at
http://www.thomsonrights.com
Any additional questions about permissions can be submitted at
thomsonrights@thomson.com

Thomson Wadsworth
10 Davis Drive
Belmont, CA 94002-3098
USA

Asia
Thomson Learning
5 Shenton Way #01-01
UIC Building
Singapore 068808

Australia/New Zealand
Thomson Learning
102 Dodds Street
Southbank, Victoria 3006
Australia

Canada
Nelson
1120 Birchmount Road
Toronto, Ontario M1K 5G4
Canada

Europe/Middle East/South Africa
Thomson Learning
High Holborn House
50/51 Bedford Row
London WC1R 4LR
United Kingdom

Latin America
Thomson Learning
Seneca, 53
Colonia Polanco
11560 Mexico D.F.
Mexico

Spain/Portugal
Paraninfo
Calle/Magallanes, 25
28015 Madrid, Spain

CONTENTS

Introduction

This book is a supplement; it is not a substitute. It will not and cannot substitute for reading and studying the textbook, attending class, taking and reviewing class notes, periodic review, etc. Joel Samaha's text is an outstanding book, and if there are any discrepancies between the text and this supplement, go with the text.

Acknowledgments

Writing supplements based on texts written by other authors is a unique form of authorship. For a variety of reasons, the author of the excellent text on which this supplement is based, Joel Samaha, is also an author of this work. This work only restyles, repeats, reformats and restates the material in the text on which it is based. It also provides questions based on the material in the text. If this supplement goes beyond what is in the text, it cannot serve its purpose, which is to help students master the material in the text. There is plenty to learn in the text without the supplement adding to the student's responsibilities. However, any errors in this work are solely the responsibility of this author, not the responsibility of the author of the text.

The author would like to thank Megan Antrim (graduate student in criminal justice at Sul Ross State University) for her assistance in proofreading this material.

This author would like to thank Jana Davis at Wadsworth Publishing Company for her patience and assistance in putting this supplement together.

Any errors are solely the responsibility of this author.

Raymond G. Kessler,
Professor and Chair
Department of Criminal Justice
Sul Ross State University
Alpine, TX 79832

Chapter 1 First Things First: Limits, Purposes and Classifying of Criminal Law

LEARNING OBJECTIVES

After studying this chapter, students will

1. understand the limits on government ability to define crimes.
2. understand the concept of constitutional democracy.
3. become familiar with the limits on criminal punishments.
4. be able to discuss the purposes of criminal punishment.
5. see how crimes are classified and graded.
6. comprehend how criminal law operates in our federal system.
7. know the basic sources of the criminal law.
8. understand the text-case method.
9. become familiar with case citations and court opinions.
10. understand how the doctrine of precedent (stare decisis) works.
11. be able to brief a case.
12. be able to find a case in a library.

KEY TERMS AND CONCEPTS (page where definition is found is at end of definition)

Constitutional democracy—powers of the majority limited by a constitution; p. 4
Equal protection of the laws—Fifth and Fourteenth Amendment ban on certain types of discrimination; p. 5
Due process of law—Fifth and Fourteenth Amendment limits on government power; p. 5
Elements of a crime—what the prosecution must prove beyond a reasonable doubt to convict; p. 5
Actus reus—the act element of a crime; p.5
Mens rea—the mental element of a crime; p.5
Concurrence—requirement that the mental state cause the act; p. 5
Cruel and unusual punishment—banned by Eighth Amendment; p.6
Principle of limited methods—criminal law should be the last resort for social control; p. 6
Retribution—an eye for an eye; punishing criminals because they deserve it; p. 7
Culpability—blameworthiness; p. 7
General prevention—same as general deterrence; punishing criminal to deter others; p.8
Special deterrence—punishing a criminal to deter that criminal in the future; p. 8
Incapacitation—take away the criminal's ability to commit crime (usually by imprisonment); p. 8
Rehabilitation—change or reform criminals so that they do not offend again; p.8
General part of criminal law—contains principles that apply to all or most specific crimes; p. 9
Special part of criminal law—contains definitions of specific crimes; p. 9
Felony—crime punishable by at least one year in a state prison; p. 9
Misdemeanor—crime punishable by incarceration in a local jail for less than one year; p. 10
Violation—offense (usually traffic) punishable by fine only; not deemed to be a conviction; p. 10
Malum in se—behavior that is inherently wrong or wrong in itself; p.10
Malum prohibitum—behavior that is wrong or a crime only because the law so specifies; p. 10

Federal system—system where power is distributed between states (including local governments) and the federal government; p. 11
Common law crimes—criminal offenses created by courts; p. 12
Criminal codes—criminal laws passed by the legislature; p. 13
Code jurisdictions—jurisdictions that have abolished common law crimes; p. 14
Text-case book—book containing text and edited excerpts from judicial opinions; p. 15
Briefing—summarizing the main points of case; p. 19
Appellate cases/opinions—opinions written by courts explaining the outcome of an appeal; p. 16
Appellant—party bringing an appeal; p. 16
Appellee—party against whose interest an appeal is brought; p. 16
Reversed—decision of higher court overturning the decision of a lower court; p. 19
Holding—the legal rule applied to the facts of a case that leads to a decision; p. 17
Majority opinion—opinion joined by a majority of judges; establishes the precedent; p. 17
Dissenting opinion—a minority opinion that disagrees with the majority opinion; p. 17
Concurring opinion—an opinion that agrees with some or all of the majority opinion; p. 18
Precedent—a prior decision used to decide a current case under the rule of *stare decisis*; p. 18
Stare decisis—general rule that new cases must be decided consistent with prior cases; p. 18
Distinguishing a case—a prior case is not a precedent because it is somehow different from the present case; p. 19
Affirmed—higher court agrees with lower court decision as to who prevails; p. 19
Reversed and remanded—Higher court disagrees with lower court decision and sends case back to lower court for further action; p. 19

CHAPTER OUTLINE

I. There are definite legal limits on the scope of criminal law in a constitutional democracy.
- A. Criminal law in a constitutional democracy is mainly about limits on government power.
- B. A democratic form of government limits crime to crimes and punishments defined by the majority and enacted into specific statutes.
- C. U.S. and state constitutions require criminal laws to be consistent with due process, equal protection, and individual rights such as privacy.
- D. Democracy and constitutions set minimum standards; the principles of criminal liability, justification, and excuse aim at the optimum standard:
  1. Principles of liability limit criminal behavior to criminal conduct and criminal conduct causing a criminal harm.
  2. Principle of justification makes otherwise criminal behavior right when actors act out of necessity.
  3. Principle of excuse excuses criminal behavior if actors are not responsible.

II. Criminal punishments are also limited in a constitutional democracy.
- A. Punishment is limited in U.S. criminal law.
  1. U.S. Constitution, Amendment VIII, bans the infliction of cruel and unusual punishment (punishments that either inflict unnecessary pain or are disproportionate to the crime).

2. Principle of limited methods
    a. Avoid criminal punishment when noncriminal social control will suffice.
    b. Don't use a more severe criminal punishment when a less severe one will accomplish social control.

B. Criminal punishment has two purposes and is good for two things:
1. Retribution (just deserts) for past crimes.
2. Prevention of future crimes.

III. Crimes in America are legally classified and graded.

A. A response to an ancient urge to make sense out of banning and punishing antisocial behavior.

B. Three reasons to learn the basics of classifying and grading crimes:
1. States organize their criminal codes according to them.
2. It's the way professionals and scholars think about them.
3. It'll help you organize, understand, and think critically about what you're learning.

C. General and special parts of criminal law divide criminal law between the general principles and doctrines of criminal law and the applications of the general information to the definitions of specific crimes.

D. "Felony, misdemeanor, and violation" grades crimes according to punishments:
1. Capital felonies (death and life without parole).
2. Ordinary felonies (one year to life in prison).
3. Gross (6–12 months in jail), ordinary (3–9 months in jail), and petty misdemeanors (10–30 days in jail).
4. Violations (fine only, with no mark on criminal record).

E. Wrongs *mala in se* (crimes inherently evil) and *mala prohibita* (crimes only because the law says they're crimes) classify and grade crimes according to their inherent severity.

F. Grading according to subject groups crimes by the subjects they cover:
1. Crimes against the state
2. Crimes against persons
3. Crimes against property
4. Crimes against public order
5. Crimes against public morals
6. Crimes against the administration of justice

IV. There are 51 criminal codes in the American system of federalism.

A. There are fifty-one (one U.S. and fifty state) criminal codes because of our federal system of government.

B. All fifty-one codes resemble one another but they differ significantly in both definitions of crimes and severity of punishment.

V. There are numerous sources of criminal law in the U.S.

A. Official sources of U.S. criminal law
1. Constitutions (U.S. and state)

2. Common law of England and the United States
3. Criminal codes (U.S., state, and municipal ordinances)
4. Judicial decisions interpreting codes and the common law

B. Common-law origins
1. Current criminal law evolved from ancient and unwritten local English customs, which were turned into the common-law crimes (homicide, assault, robbery, burglary, and larceny) by English courts before there were legislatures.
2. As society became more complex, English courts and then English legislatures modified the list of common-law crimes and then added new crimes to the list.
3. English colonists brought the common law with them to the American colonies; after the Revolution, the new states passed "reception statutes" adopting the common law as their own.
4. Many times since the Revolution, reform movements have tried to abolish the court-created common-law crimes and replace them with codes passed by majorities in state legislatures and signed by elected state governors.
5. Today, we have so-called code states and common-law states. That's the formal side of criminal law. Informally, the common-law definitions of crimes and the common-law defenses to crime still have a powerful influence on U.S. state criminal law.

VI. The text-case method is used in this and other books to teach about the law.

A. Two parts of book
1. Text defines and explains concepts and principles.
2. Case excerpts test your understanding (and get you to think critically by applying definitions, concepts, and principles to real cases).

B. Precedent and *stare decisis*
1. Judges use prior decisions to decide present cases.
2. Judges are very reluctant to get off the beaten path of precedent.
3. Changing needs and times and prior mistakes encourage judges occasionally to overcome their resistance to stay on the beaten path of precedent.

CHAPTER SUMMARY

America is a constitutional democracy. The power of the majority or the government to criminalize and punish behavior is limited by the U.S. Constitution. For instance, the Eighth Amendment prohibits punishments that are cruel and unusual.

The three basic elements of most crimes are *actus reus, mens rea* and concurrence. There are three elements, and any others must be proven by the government beyond a reasonable doubt. The *actus reus* is the criminal act. The *mens rea* is the criminal intent. The concurrence requirement is that that the criminal intent must trigger or cause the criminal act.

Use of the criminal sanction should also be limited by the principle of limited methods. This means that the criminal law should be used as a last resort when other informal and governmental solutions do not work.

Utilization of the criminal law should also be guided by careful consideration of the purposes of criminal punishment. The oldest purpose or justification is retribution. This is the idea of an eye for an eye. Criminals should be hated and pay their debt to society. Other purposes are preventive in nature. They aim to prevent crime. Prevention or deterrence is of two types.
In general deterrence we punish an offender to deter the public from committing such crimes.
In special deterrence we punish this offender to deter this offender. Incapacitation involves imprisonment, death or chemical change so that the offender will be unable to commit another crime. Finally, rehabilitation aims at changing, curing or reforming the offender to eliminate his or her future crimes.

Crimes can be classified or graded according to many schemes. The most common are felony or misdemeanor. Typically a crime is a felony if it is punishable by at least one year in a state prison. Misdemeanors are punishable by one year or less in a local jail. Some crimes cover behavior that is *malum in se*, which means bad in itself or inherently evil. Murder, rape and robbery are examples. Other crimes cover behavior that is unlawful only because the law says it is. These are called *malum prohibitum*. Crimes can also be classified according to the subject or the value that is harmed. Examples would be crimes against persons, property, public order, public morals and the administration of justice.

The criminal law itself can be divided into two parts. The special part of the criminal law provides the definitions of various crimes. The general part provides general principles that apply to all offenses. This would include *mens rea* provisions and accomplice liability provisions.

The Constitution establishes a federal system for America. Power is shared and divided between the states and the federal government. Thus, both the states (and cities and counties) and the federal government can pass criminal laws. We thus have 50 sets of state criminal laws and separate federal criminal laws. Although there are some basic concepts in common, there are many differences among these 51 jurisdictions.

The U.S. Constitution is the Supreme law of the land and is the ultimate source and limitation on criminal law. Each state also has a constitution that can limit that state's criminal law. Some states still allow courts to create common law crimes in addition to state criminal statutes. These states are referred to as common-law jurisdictions. Around half of the states do not have common law crimes. Crimes are created by the legislature in the form of statutes. These are called code jurisdictions. The federal government passes criminal statues and cities and counties can also create crimes. The final source of criminal law is court decisions either creating common law crimes or interpreting statutes or constitutions.

America's legal system and its criminal law have their origins in British history prior to the American Revolution. The first crimes in England were common law crimes such as rape and murder. The common law then was the judge-made law based on the common customs of the people of England. Over time, English common law was supplemented by statutes.

After the Revolution, America adopted much of English common law. However, over time, statutory criminal law has replaced common law crimes. Judge-made law (common law) was criticized as being disorderly, incomplete and anti-democratic. About half the states no longer permit courts to create new crimes. Such states have created Crimes/Criminal/Penal Codes. Development of these codes was facilitated by the work of the American Law Institute's Model Penal Code Committee. This committee studied, recommended and published a Model Penal Code to guide legislators in updating their criminal law. The Model Penal Code has been very valuable for judges, legislators, scholars and students. Many states have adopted parts of the Model Penal Code.

This textbook uses the text-case method. It includes explanatory text and excerpts from court cases/opinions. Generally, only appellate courts write opinions. The party who appeals is called the appellant. The party whose victory in the court below is being challenged is called the appellee.

When reading case opinions or excerpts, students need to be able to find the various parts of cases. Only the majority opinion establishes the law and the precedent. There may also be concurring and dissenting (disagreeing) opinions. Probably the two most important are the holding and the rationale. The holding is the legal rule announced by the court that decides the case. The reasoning is the reasons underlying the holding. Both of these are utilized in the process of *stare decisis*.

Courts in America are generally expected to follow prior decisions called precedents and apply the doctrine of *stare decisis*. New cases should be decided in a fashion consistent with the prior cases or precedents. This helps provide predictability and stability in the law. However, *stare decisis* is just a general rule; there are exceptions. A possible precedent can be avoided by distinguishing it. It is argued that there is a significant difference between the prior case and the older case that makes the older case inappropriate as a precedent for the new case.

Students should also be able to find court cases and opinions. This is usually done through the opinion citation system. An example of a citation would be U.S. v. Jones 453 U.S. 272 (1972). The names of the parties are given first. The first number (453) is the volume number. The abbreviation (U.S.) is the set of books or reporters. In this case, U.S. refers to United States Reports, which is the official U.S. Supreme Court publication. The second number (272) is the page in that volume where that opinion begins. Finally, the last number is the date (1972) the opinion was handed down. There are a variety of publication and reporters for different jurisdictions. Some citations will also indicate the particular court that handed down the opinion in the same parentheses as the date.

PRACTICE TEST BANK

1. Criminal law and punishment should be limited by consideration of their _____.
   a. purposes
   b. conjunctions
   c. attributions
   d. connotations

2. The U.S. Constitution _____.
   a. limits the power of government to criminalize and punish
   b. is subject to the limitations imposed by state constitutions
   c. can be amended like any statute
   d. can be limited by treaty

3. The term *actus reus* means _____.
   a. evil mind
   b. intent triggered act
   c. blameworthiness
   d. criminal act

4. The term *mens rea* means _____.
   a. blameworthiness
   b. criminal act
   c. criminal intent
   d. concurrence

5. The concurrence requirement is that the _____.
   a. criminal intent must trigger the act
   b. the act must trigger the criminal intent
   c. act and harm must trigger the intent
   d. harm and intent must trigger the act

6. The three main legal categories of defenses to crime are _____.
   a. mental, physical and emotional
   b. incompetency, insanity and intent
   c. act, intent and concurrence
   d. justifications, excuses and alibis

7. Which of the amendments contains the ban on cruel and unusual punishment?
   a. 4th
   b. 8th
   c. 9th
   d. 10th

8. According to the principle of limited methods, the criminal law _____.
   a. must conform to constitutional requirements
   b. should be utilized only after other methods fail
   c. must give fair notice as to what constitutes a crime
   d. should reflect the will of the majority

9. Murder, manslaughter, rape, burglary and arson were among the common law _____.
   a. misdemeanors
   b. criminal statutes
   c. violations
   d. felonies

10. In a constitutional democracy, _____.
    a. the power of the majority or government is limited by a constitution
    b. there is no limit on the power of the majority
    c. ordinary legislation takes precedence over the constitution
    d. the executive branch is the dominant branch

11. An eye for an eye approach to punishment is consistent with _____.
    a. general deterrence
    b. special deterrence
    c. incapacitation
    d. retribution

12. Retribution logically requires that the criminal be _____.
    a. blameworthy or culpable
    b. capable of change and wanting to change
    c. a potential re-offender or threat to society
    d. predictably dangerous or potentially dangerous

13. Many criminologists reject the most basic assumption of retribution, which is _____.
    a. determinism
    b free will
    c. cognition
    d. adaptability

14. The idea of _____ involves confinement, surgical alteration or execution to prevent further crimes by that defendant.
    a. rehabilitation
    b. special deterrence
    c. incapacitation
    d. retribution

15. The legal principles that apply to all crimes (e.g., defenses) are called the _____ part of the criminal law.
  a. general
  b. miscellaneous
  c. concurrent
  d. specific

16. The part of the criminal law that provides the elements of various particular crimes is called the _____ part.
  a. specific
  b. special
  c. specious
  d. spandrel

17. In most jurisdictions, a felony is defined as a crime that is punishable by incarceration of at least ____ year(s) in a prison.
  a. one
  b. two
  c. three
  d. five

18. Crimes such as murder and rape, which involve inherently evil conduct, are termed ____.
  a. *malum prohibitum.*
  b. *malum in se.*
  c. *incorporatum.*
  d. *excelsis.*

19 Many modern penal codes classify crimes in terms of the subject (e.g., crimes against property, person, etc.). This classification involves the _____.
  a. interest or value harmed
  b. amount of social harm
  c. culpability of the offender
  d. harm or damage to a particular victim

20. Which of the following statements is most accurate regarding the criminal law in the U.S.?
  a. There is very little variation between jurisdictions because all states have adopted most of the Model Penal Code.
  b. There is very little variation between jurisdictions because all jurisdictions must conform to the U.S. Constitution and U.S. Supreme Court decision.
  c. For a number of reasons, there is significant variation among jurisdictions in the U.S.
  d. Because of the Eighth Amendment, there are some differences between jurisdictions.

21. Under the principle of federalism, government power is allocated between _____.
   a. state (and local) governments and the federal government
   b. the federal government and the United Nations
   c. state and local governments
   d. state government and the United Nations

22. In the U.S. today, most criminal law is _____ law.
   a. federal
   b. state
   c. county
   d. international

23 American criminal law has its origin in English _____.
   a. civil law
   b. code law
   c. common law
   d. royal decrees

24. Crimes/Criminal/Penal Codes are created by _____.
   a. legislative bodies
   b. judges
   c. executive officials
   d. international organizations

25. Today, at least half the states have _____.
   a. retained common law crimes as their only crimes
   b. abolished common law crimes
   c. recognized common law, statutory and international crimes
   d. abolished their penal/criminal/crimes codes

26. A code jurisdiction is one that has _____.
   a. retained common law crimes as their only crimes
   b. abolished common law crimes
   c. recognized common law, statutory and international crimes
   d. abolished their penal/criminal/crimes codes

27. Most states and the federal government have ____ levels of appellate courts.
   a. two
   b. three
   c. four
   d. five

28. In a court case/opinion title the first named party is the party who brought the appeal, the _____.
    a. appellee
    b. appellor
    c. appellony
    d. appellant

29. In a court case/opinion, the legal rule that decides the case is called the _____.
    a. issue
    b. holding
    c. judgment
    d. reasoning

30. The established law of the case and the precedent is established in the _____ opinion.
    a. dominant
    b. concurring
    c. majority
    d. plurality

True-False

1. Prior decisions that are relevant to deciding the current case are called precedents.
    a. true
    b. false

2. The doctrine of *stare decisis* generally requires judges to follow precedents established by equal or higher courts.
    a. true
    b. false

3. One way for a court to avoid a possible precedent is to distinguish the prior case.
    a. true
    b. false

4. The second set of numbers in a case/opinion citation is the date of the decision.
    a. true
    b. false

5. The first set of numbers in a case citation is the page number on which the case begins.
    a. true
    b. false

6. Most criminal laws in the U.S. are state laws.
    a. true
    b. false

7. Rehabilitation and prevention are prospective (looking to prevent future crime).
   a. true
   b. false

8. Principles of accomplice liability are a part of the special part of the criminal law.
   a. true
   b. false

9. Crimes which are *malum in se* are more harmful and blameworthy than crimes which are *malum prohibitum*.
   a. true
   b. false

10. The federal government and most states utilize common law crimes exclusively.
   a. true
   b. false

11. *Stare decisis* is an absolute rule with no exceptions.
   a. true
   b. false

12. In a constitutional democracy, the constitution limits the power of the majority.
   a. true
   b. false

13. The term *actus reus* refers to the criminal act.
   a. true
   b. false

14. The term *mens rea* refers to the criminal intent.
   a. true
   b. false

15. The concurrence element of a crime requires that the act trigger the mental state.
   a. true
   b. false

16. The Sixth Amendment bans cruel and unusual punishment.
   a. true
   b. false

17. The ban on cruel and unusual punishment requires that punishment be proportional to the offense.
   a. true
   b. false

18. American criminal law is based on the common law of Spain.
    a. true
    b. false

19. Punishing an individual to deter him or her from committing more crimes is called specific deterrence.
    a. true
    b. false

20. The elements of the crime of rape or murder would be found in the special part of the criminal law.
    a. true
    b. false

21. Felonies are crimes punishable by more than one year of incarceration in a local jail.
    a. true
    b. false

22. All states have the death penalty for certain kinds of murders.
    a. true
    b. false

23 Driving on the left side of the road is an example of an offense that is *malum prohibitum*.
    a. true
    b. false

24. Sodomy was not a common law crime.
    a. true
    b. false

25 Code jurisdictions are those that have kept common law offenses.
    a. true
    b. false

<u>Fill in the blank</u>

1. Sets of three dots in a writing indicating that some material from quoted material has been omitted are called ________________.

2. The party who appeals an adverse judgment or decision is called the ________________.

3. The most common type of collateral attack on a conviction is ____________________.

4. The general principle that courts must follow the law established in the precedents is ______________________________.

5. If a judge decides that a prior case is not a precedent because it is different in some significant way from the current case, we call this ________________ cases.

6. When an appellate court agrees with the decision of the court immediately below it, we say it has ________________ the lower court decision.

7. When a case is ________________, it is sent back down to a lower court for further proceedings in accordance with the appellate court's decision.

8. In the citation 319 U.S. 432, the 319 is the ________________ number.

9. The purposes of *stare decisis* and ________________ are to give the law stability and predictability.

10. Torture is prohibited by the ________________ Amendment.

11. The ________________ part of the criminal law specifies principles that apply to all crimes.

12. A felony offense for which death is authorized is a called a ________________ felony.

13. Larceny, arson, burglary and theft are classified as crimes against ________________.

14. Judge-made law originally based on the common customs or traditions of the people is called the ________________ law.

15. Today, most new crimes are created by the legislature by passing ________________.

<u>Essay</u>

1. Describe, define, compare and contrast common law crimes and statutory crimes.

2. Discuss the arguments for and against courts having the power to create crimes. Explain your position on the matter.

3. List and define the seven main sources of criminal law. Give an example of each.

4. Describe, define, compare and contrast common law and code jurisdictions.

5. Define and discuss retribution and the various preventive purposes (justifications) for criminal punishment. Provide examples of each. Which do you think should be the dominant purpose? Explain your position.

CHAPTER 1 ANSWER KEY (the number in parentheses after the answer is the page in the text where the answer can be found)

Multiple Choice

1—a (6)	2—a (6)	3—d (5)	4—c (5)	5—a (6)
6—d (6)	7—b (8)	8—b (6)	9—d (12)	10—a (4)
11—d (7)	12—a (7)	13—b (8)	14—c (8)	15—a (9)
16—b (9)	17—a (10)	18—b (10)	19—a (11)	20—c (11)
21—a (11)	22—b (12)	23—c (12)	24—a (13)	25—b (14)
26—a (16)	27—a (16)	28—d (16)	29—b (17)	30—c (17)

True-False

1—T (18)	2—T (18)	3—T (19)	4—F (20)	5—F (20)
6—T (12)	7—T (8)	8—F (9)	9—T (10)	10—F (13)
11—F (18)	12—T (4)	13—T (5)	14—T (5)	15—F (5)
16—F (6)	17—T (6)	18—F (12)	19—F (8)	20—T (9)
21—F (10)	22—F (10)	23—T (10)	24—F (12)	25—F (14)

Fill in the blank

1—ellipses (15)	2—appellant(16)	3—*habeas corpus* (16)	4—*stare decisis*(18)
5—distinguishing (19)	6—affirmed (19)	7—remanded (19)	8—volume (20)
9—precedent (18)	10—Eighth (6)	11—general (9)	12—capital (10)
13—property (11)	14—common (12)	15—statutes (13)	

Chapter 2 Constitutional Limits on Criminal Law

LEARNING OBJECTIVES

After studying this chapter, students will

1. understand how the constitution limits the scope of the criminal law.
2. be familiar with the concept of the rule of law.
3. know the definition and examples of *ex post facto* laws.
4. understand the void-for-vagueness doctrine.
5. understand the concept of equal protection of the law.
6. be able to discuss freedom of speech and press.
7. be familiar with the constitutional right to privacy.
8. understand the majority and dissenting opinions in Lawrence v. Texas (2003).
9. know the various dimensions of the ban on cruel and unusual punishment.

KEY TERMS AND CONCEPTS

Rule of law—can punish only if there is a specific law defining the crime and its punishment; p. 27
Principle of legality—same as rule of law; p. 27
Ex post facto law—retroactive criminal law; p. 27
Arbitrary law enforcement—enforcement without reason or standards; p. 27
Void-for-vagueness doctrine—due process limit outlawing extremely vague laws; p. 27
Rational basis—reasonableness test under equal protection for most classifications; p. 32
Strict scrutiny—high burden on government to justify classifications on race, ethnicity, etc.; p. 32
Heightened scrutiny—scrutiny higher than rational basis, lower than strict; for gender discrimination; p. 32
Fundamental right—infringement or classification thereon must meet strict scrutiny test; a right with preferred status; p. 35
Obscenity—offensive, sexually explicit material not protected by First Amendment; p. 35
Profanity—irreverence toward sacred things; protected by First Amendment; p. 35
Libel—defamation in print; p. 35
Slander—defamation by spoken word; p. 35
Fighting words—words likely to incite immediate violence in another; p. 35
Clear and present danger—one test for dangerous speech that the government can punish; p. 35
Void-for-over breadth doctrine—restrictions on speech that sweep too broadly and deter protected speech; p. 36
Barbaric punishments—brutality and torture; banned by Eighth Amendment; p. 48
Principle of proportionality—Eight Amendment requirement that punishment fit the crime; p. 48

CHAPTER OUTLINE

I. The Rule of law (part of our system of constitutional democracy) limits government power and majority rule.

II. *Ex post facto* laws are banned by the Constitution. They are banned to
   A. Give fair warning to private individuals
   B. Prevent arbitrary government action

III. Vague laws are also banned under the due process (void-for-vagueness) doctrine.
   A. Limited to laws that are vague to reasonable individuals and officers, not subjectively unreasonable (specific individuals and officers in the case).
   B. Deprive individuals of life, liberty, and property without due process.
   C. This affects all laws to some extent, because words can never have the precise meaning of numbers.
   D. Carry a heavy burden of proof for defendants in challenges.

IV. The U.S. Constitution, Article XIV, requirement of equal protection doesn't compel government to treat all people exactly alike.
   A. Criminal statutes that reasonably classify people differently don't violate the equal protection guarantee.
   B. Classifications in criminal statutes based on race and ethnicity are never reasonable.
   C. Gender classifications are suspect but not always unreasonable.
   D. Age classifications are examined for reasonableness.

V. The First Amendment guarantee of free speech is a preferred right (preferred status).
   A. Free speech includes nonverbal expressive conduct.
   B. Speech doesn't include all words and expressive conduct (obscenity, profanity, libel and slander, and fighting words).
   C. Excluded or unprotected expression can be made a crime, depending on the time, place, and manner of the expression.
   D. Hate speech can be made a crime, depending on the circumstances.

VI. According to U.S. Supreme Court, the U.S. Constitution guarantees an implied fundamental right to privacy.
   A. Right to privacy derives from several amendments to the U.S. Constitution or from word "liberty" in due process clauses.
   B. U.S. Supreme Court had previously strictly limited the right to the home, family life, procreation, and child rearing.
   C. In Lawrence v. Texas (2003), the right is extended to cover private, adult, consensual homosexual conduct.

VII. U.S. Constitution, Amendment VIII, bans cruel and unusual punishments.
   A. Unnecessary infliction of pain
   B. Punishments disproportionate to the crime committed
   C. Death (at least for intentional murder) is not cruel and unusual punishment

CHAPTER SUMMARY

The Founding Fathers were realists who recognized the threat to individual liberty from an unlimited democracy and unlimited government. The United States is a *constitutional* democracy. The desires of the majority are controlled by provisions of the U.S. and state constitutions

The purposes of banning *ex post facto* and vague criminal statutes are to give fair warning to individuals as to what the law prohibits and to prevent arbitrary enforcement by public officials. The constitutional basis for banning laws so vague that reasonable private individuals and public officials can't understand them is that such laws deprive individuals of life, liberty, or property without due process of law.

The U.S. Constitution doesn't guarantee that criminal laws treat everybody exactly alike; it does command that classifying people or behavior differently be reasonable. Classifications based on race and ethnicity are almost never reasonable.

Under the U.S. Constitution, Amendment I, the guarantee of free speech is a fundamental right. Government action that infringes on rights that are deemed fundamental must be shown to be more than reasonable. The action must be justified by showing that it furthers a compelling governmental interest. According to the U.S. Supreme Court, some kinds of non-verbal expressive conduct are speech; some words aren't "speech;" and some speech isn't protected by the guarantee of free speech. Obscenity and fighting words are types of speech that are not protected by the First Amendment.

The word "privacy" doesn't appear in the U.S. Constitution, but the U.S. Supreme Court has based an implied right to privacy in several Amendments to the U.S. Constitution. The U.S. Supreme Court has narrowly confined the right to privacy to homes, traditional forms of family life, reproduction, and child rearing. Whether or not the right to privacy protects private, adult consensual homosexual conduct is a controversial issue. In Bowers v. Hardwick (1986) the Court held that it was not protected. Bowers v. Hardwick was overruled in 2003 in Lawrence v. Texas.

The U.S. Supreme Court has interpreted the ban on cruel and unusual punishments to include barbaric punishments and punishments disproportionate to crimes. The death penalty is valid if certain constitutional rules are followed.

PRACTICE TEST BANK

Multiple Choice

1. The U.S. is a _____.
   a. constitutional monarchy
   b. pure democracy
   c. parliamentary style government
   d. constitutional democracy

2. Which of the following would violate the ban on *ex post facto* laws?
   a. retroactive criminal statute
   b. vague statute giving too much power to government
   c. statute broadly regulating protective speech
   d. providing death penalty for petty theft

3. The rule of law and principle of legality require that people be punished only _____.
   a. for violating properly enacted laws
   b. if they had some culpable *mens rea*
   c. if they personally did the criminal act
   d. if their acts harm society

4. Which of the following are consistent with Madison's famous quote cited in the text?
   a. Governments are rarely required in society.
   b. Some form of government is necessary.
   c. Government should not have the power to control people.
   d. Government should be abolished as soon as feasible.

5. Which of the following are consistent with Madison's famous quote presented in the text?
   a. The federal government should be trusted with wide-ranging powers.
   b. Constitutional limits can be disregarded when it is in the public interest.
   c. People exercising government power may attempt to abuse that power.
   d. The need for government will eventually fade away.

6. Which of the following is most consistent with the paradox or problem posed in Madison's famous quote presented in the text?
   a. Government is necessary to control people, but some of these people will become the government, and must be given enough power to benefit society, but not enough power to create tyranny.
   b. As government improves the morality and ethics of people, the need for a government to control them will decrease.
   c. We can rely on the people to elect officials who will not abuse their power.
   d. The people must trust the government to do the right thing and the government must trust the people to do the right things. Therefore, the U.S. Constitution can be a relatively short document.

7. Which of the following is most consistent with Madison's view of human nature as expressed in the quote presented in the text?
   a. Human beings are basically good and should be given the benefit of the doubt as both citizens and public officials.
   b. Each generation of Americans will become more wise and altruistic.
   c. There is a dark side to human nature that must be controlled.
   d. Human nature is perfectible, and it is the primary duty of government to help individuals realize their own strengths.

8. The primary considerations in analysis of laws under the void for vagueness doctrine are _____.
   a. retroactivity and potential for punishing innocent people
   b. legislative encroachment on the judiciary and legislative tyranny
   c. infringement of First and Seventh Amendment rights
   d. reasonably fair notice and potential for arbitrary or discriminator enforcement

9. In a constitutional democracy, _____.
   a. the will of the majority is the supreme law
   b. the power of the majority and government are limited by the Constitution
   c. the legislature has the final say on the meaning of the Constitution
   d. the Constitution can be amended just like any statute

10. The _____ Amendment requires that states provide equal protection of the laws.
   a. First
   b. Sixth
   c. Eighth
   d. Fourteenth

11. Except when dealing with fundamental rights and classifying by race, ethnicity, gender, etc., the government can meet an equal protection challenge to a law by _____.
   a. passing the strict scrutiny test
   b. meeting the requirement of heightened scrutiny
   c. showing that the law has a rational basis
   d. showing that the law furthers a compelling governmental interest

12. The first Amendment offers protection from government for _____.
   a. some expressive conduct as well as some spoken or written words
   b. every form of spoken or written word
   c. every form of expressive conduct
   c. some spoken or written words but no expressive conduct

13. Which of the following types of speech is protected by the First Amendment?
    a. obscenity
    b. libel and slander of a private citizen
    c. fighting words
    d. criticism of government

14. Statutes which ban some forms of unprotected speech but which ____ the exercise of some protected speech may be unconstitutional under the overbreadth doctrine.
    a. chill or deter
    b. can lead to arbitrary enforcement against
    c. promote or facilitate
    d. condone or ratify

15. In People v. Rokicki (1999), the defendant argued he was being unconstitutionally punished for his beliefs. The Illinois Supreme Court stated that the defendant's First Amendment challenge to the hate crime law was _____.
    a. invalid because he allowed his beliefs to motivate unreasonable conduct
    b. upheld because he was being punished because of his beliefs
    c. invalid because his beliefs were totally irrelevant to the case
    d. upheld because his conduct did not go beyond mere expression

16. In Texas v. Johnson (1989), the Court held that burning an American flag as part of a political protest could _____.
    a. be punished because it involved conduct
    b. be punished because the American flag is a unique symbol
    c. not be punished because it was protected expressive conduct
    d. not be punished because it was pure speech

17. Even thought the word "_____" does not appear anywhere in the U.S. Constitution, the U.S. Supreme Court has held that there is such a fundamental right.
    a. liberty
    b. privacy
    c. property
    d. attainder

18. In Lawrence v. Texas (2003), the U.S. Supreme Court _____ its prior decision in Bowers v. Hardwick (1986).
    a. affirmed
    b. reversed
    c. overruled
    d. remanded

19. The ban on cruel and unusual punishment is found in the _____ Amendment.
   a. Fifth
   b. Sixth
   c. Seventh
   d. Eighth

20. In State v. Wilson (1996), the Louisiana Supreme Court distinguished the U.S. Supreme Court's decision in Coker v. Georgia (1997) because the Wilson case involved _____.
   a. the death of a child
   b. the rape of a child
   c. a child killing another child
   d. a child raping another child

21. In State v. Wilson (1996), the Louisiana Supreme Court stated that retribution is _____.
   a. a proper goal of the criminal sanction because private revenge (self-help) is not permitted
   b. a proper goal because it will deter offenders
   c. not a proper goal because society evolved beyond the barbaric goal of retribution
   d. not a proper goal because only courts can determine the proper goal of punishment

22. In Lawrence v. Texas (2003) the majority stated that the fact that a majority of the people _____ is by itself not a valid basis for a criminal law.
   a. voted for the law in a referendum
   b. feel the conduct is immoral
   c. have not personally engaged in such behavior
   d. are not as enlightened as the Court

23. In Lawrence v. Texas (2003) the Court _____ the principle of *stare decisis.*
   a. followed
   b. refused to follow
   c. held that it would no longer feel any allegiance to
   d. allowed a federal statute to overcome

24. In Lawrence v. Texas, the Court held that the state could not punish the homosexual behavior involved because such laws _____.
   a. violate equal protection since it was not applied against females
   b. demean the existence and control the destiny of homosexuals
   c. violate equal protection because homosexuals are not allowed to marry in Texas
   d. are contrary to international law

25. The dissenters in Lawrence v. Texas (2003) stated that the majority _____.
   a. had misconstrued the meaning of equal protection
   b. wrongly failed to overrule Bowers v. Hardwick
   c. adopted the politically correct position in the culture war
   d. wrongly overruled Roe v. Wade

26. In Roe v. Wade (1973) and Lawrence v. Texas (2003) the Court found the source of the right to privacy in _____.
    a. the penumbras of a number of specific constitutional rights
    b. the equal protection clause
    c. the Ninth Amendment
    d. substantive due process

27. Punishments which are _____ to the harm or crime committed are cruel and unusual.
    a. disjunctive
    b. disproportionate
    c. disassociated
    d. disconsolate

28. In Robinson v. California (1962) the Court held that punishing ____was cruel and unusual punishment.
    a. a person for being addicted to the use of narcotics
    b. an alcoholic for public drunkenness
    c. a kleptomaniac for theft
    d. a nymphomaniac for public indecency

29. Which of the following means of execution is not cruel and unusual punishment?
    a. crucifixion
    b. beheading
    c. electrocution
    d. drawing and quartering

30. Justice Thomas, dissenting in Lawrence v. Texas, agreed with former Justice Stewart that the U.S. Constitution contains no _____.
    a. equal protection clause
    b. requirements for procedural due process
    c. Fourth Amendment right to privacy
    d. general substantive due process right to privacy

<u>True-False</u>

1. The authors of the U.S. Constitution and Bill of Rights were suspicious of government power.
    a. true
    b. false

2. Under the principle of legality a person can be criminally punished only if there was in place at the time a properly enacted law and corresponding punishment.
    a. true
    b. false

3. The ban on *ex post facto* laws is designed to prevent excessively vague laws.
   a. true
   b. false

4. The void-for-vagueness doctrine totally prohibits any vagueness or uncertainty in laws.
   a. true
   b. false

5. Laws involving gender classifications are tested under the rational basis test.
   a. true
   b. false

6. Fighting words are not protected by the First Amendment.
   a. true
   b. false

7. Fighting words are specifically defined as words that create a clear and present danger of an evil that legislatures have a right to prevent.
   a. true
   b. false

8. Libel and slander are types of defamation.
   a. true
   b. false

9. Libel is written while slander is spoken.
   a. true
   b. false

10. In Stanley v. Georgia, the U.S. Supreme Court struck down a statute criminalizing personal adult possession of obscene materials in the privacy of the home.
    a. true
    b. false

11. In Lawrence v. Texas (2003), the Court held that the Texas homosexual conduct law violated equal protection because it discriminated against same-sex couples.
    a. true
    b. false

12. The Sixth Amendment prohibits cruel and unusual punishment.
    a. true
    b. false

13. A majority of the U.S. Supreme Court has consistently agreed that the proportionality principle applies to the death penalty.
    a. true
    b. false

14. The term arbitrary means without reason or standards.
    a. true
    b. false

15. Equal protection requires that government treat everyone equally.
    a. true
    b. false

16. Under equal protection, racial classifications in laws are subject to strict scrutiny.
    a. true
    b. false

17. Under equal protection, age classifications are subject to strict scrutiny.
    a. true
    b. false

18. Freedom of speech is found in the First Amendment.
    a. true
    b. false

19 All types of speech and press are protected by the First Amendment.
    a. true
    b. false

20. Expressive conduct is not protected by the First Amendment.
    a. true
    b. false

21. Fighting words are not protected by the First Amendment.
    a. true
    b. false

22. Freedom of speech and expression are fundamental rights.
    a. true
    b. false

23. Broadly written laws that have an impact on protected speech and press are invalid if they are deemed overbroad.
    a. true
    b. false

24. Hate crimes violate the First Amendment.
    a. true
    b. false

25. The death penalty always violates the Eighth Amendment.
    a. true
    b. false

<u>Fill in the blank</u>

1. The Eighth Amendment principle of _______________ requires that punishments fit the crime.

2. _______________ is offensive, sexually explicit material which is not protected by the First Amendment.

3. _______________ words are words that are likely to provoke the average person to retaliate physically, thus causing a breach of the peace.

4. Defamation expressed in print is termed _______________.

5. _______________ is defamation by spoken words.

6. Making a statement through acts or symbols is called _______________ conduct.

7. The _______________ Amendment states that we have rights in addition to those specifically mentioned in the Bill of Rights.

8. Government classifications on the basis of race are subject to ____________________ by the courts.

9. In _______________ (1962), the court used the ban on cruel and unusual punishment to invalidate a law making it a crime to be addicted to the use of narcotics.

10. In _______________, the Court refused to expand the right to privacy to cover private, consensual, adult homosexual conduct.

11. The constitutional right to privacy was first announced by the Court in 1965 in _______________.

12. Freedom of speech and press are found in the _______________ Amendment.

13. The Equal Protection clause is found in the _______________ Amendment.

14. The right of privacy was extended to cover a woman's abortion decision in 1973 in _______________.

15. The American form of government is described as a constitutional _______________.

Essay

1. Trace and discuss the development of the constitutional right to privacy from Griswold v. Connecticut (1965) to Lawrence v. Texas (2003).

2. What points was Madison trying to make in his famous quote about men, government and angels? Do you agree or disagree with the quote? To what extent does American government today reflect the tension described in the quote? Be sure to provide examples.

3. Define, discuss, compare and contrast, the void-for-vagueness, void-for-overbreadth and *ex post facto* law concepts. Provide examples of each.

4. Discuss and describe the U.S. Supreme Court's decision in Lawrence v. Texas (2003). Do you agree or disagree with the majority? Be sure to explain your position.

5. Define, discuss, compare and contrast a pure and a constitutional democracy. Be sure to provide examples. Which of these two do you prefer as a form of government? Be sure to explain your position.

CHAPTER 2 ANSWER KEY

Multiple Choice

1—d (26)	2—a (27)	3—a (27)	4—b (26)	5—c (26)
6—a (26)	7—c (26)	8—d (28)	9—b (26)	10—d (31
11—c (32)	12—a (35)	13—d (35)	14—a (36)	15—a (38
16—c (40)	17—b (41)	18—c (46)	19—d (48)	20—b (50)
21—a (50)	22—b (45)	23—b (46)	24—b (45)	25—c (46)
26—d (26)	27—b (48)	28—a (49)	29—c (48)	30—d (47)

True-False

1—T (26)	2—T (27)	3—F (27)	4—F (28)	5—F (32)
6—T (35)	7—F (35)	8—T (35)	9—T (35)	10—T (42)
11—F (46)	12—F (48)	13—T (49)	14—T (27)	15—F (31)
16—T (32)	17—F (33)	18—T (35)	19—F (35)	20—F (30)
21—T (35)	22—T (35)	23—T (36)	24—F (39)	25—F (48)

Fill in the blank

1—proportionality (48)	2—obscenity (35)	3—fighting (35)	4—libel (35)
5—slander (35)	6—expressive (35)	7—Ninth (41)	8—strict scrutiny(32)
9—Robinson v. California (41)	10—Bowers v. Hardwick (43)	11—Griswold v. Connecticut (41)	
12—First (35)	13—Fourteenth (31)	14—Roe v. Wade (43)	15—democracy (26)

Chapter 3 The General Principles of Criminal Liability

LEARNING OBJECTIVES

After studying this chapter, student will

1. be familiar with the basic principles of criminal liability.
2. know the requirement of an *actus reus.*
3. understand why acts must be voluntary to be criminal.
4. understand how possession is an act.
5. be familiar with the two types of possession.
6. understand the difference between knowing and mere possession.

5. know why a status or condition cannot be a criminal act.
6. know that an omission to act can also be a criminal act.
7. be familiar with the two common criminal forms of omission, failures to report and intervene.
8. know that an omission to act can be a crime only when there is a duty to act.

KEY WORDS AND CONCEPTS

Actual possession—having an object on one's person or within reach and control; p. 78
Actus reus—Latin term for the criminal act; p.55
American bystander rule—rule in most American jurisdictions that, in general, there is not legal duty to aid a stranger in peril; p. 68
Elements of crime—what the prosecution must prove to get a conviction; p.55
Mens rea—mental element of a crime; p. 55
Concurrence—element of crime requiring act to flow from *mens rea*; p.55
Automatism—mental state in which acts are not voluntary or conscious; p. 59
Somnambulism—sleepwalking; acts during this state are not voluntary; p. 59
Criminal omission—failure to act that can constitute the act element of a crime; p. 67
Failure to report—one form of omission that is sometimes criminalized; p. 67
Failure to intervene—one form of omission that is sometimes criminalized; p. 67
Legal duty—duty imposed by law, including statute, common law or contract; p.67
Good Samaritan doctrine—legal duty to aid strangers in peril; p. 68
Manifest criminality—intentions must be manifested acts; intentions alone not criminal; p. 58
Status—condition; p. 63
American bystander rule—generally no legal duty to aid those in peril; p. 68
Legal fiction—legal assumption that something is a fact, when it not; p. 77
Constructive possession—item is not on person or nearby, but it is under person's control; p. 78
Knowing possession—knowing the nature of the thing possessed; p. 78
Mere possession—possessing something without knowing what it is; p.78

CHAPTER OUTLINE

I. There are a number of general principles of criminal liability.
- A. The government must prove every element of the crime beyond a reasonable doubt.
- B. The Constitution requires a criminal act to prove criminal liability.
  - 1. A criminal act is the basis of the principle of *actus reus*.
  - 2. This is an element the prosecution has to prove beyond a reasonable doubt.
- C. Two types of crimes lead to criminal liability.
  - 1. Criminal conduct requires proving three elements of crimes.
    - a. *Actus reus* (criminal act)
    - b. *Mens rea* (criminal intent)
    - c. Concurrence (criminal act triggered by criminal intent)
  - 2. Criminal conduct causing criminal harm requires proving five elements of crimes.
    - a. *Actus reus*
    - b. *Mens rea*
    - c. Concurrence
      - (1) *Actus reus* and *mens rea* produce criminal conduct.
      - (2) The criminal conduct results in harm.
    - d. Causation (must prove the criminal conduct produced criminal harm as defined in the criminal statute)
    - e. Resulting harm (the specific result defined in the criminal code)
- D. Each element of crime relates to a general principle of criminal liability.

II. Every crime involves a criminal act, referred to as the *actus reus*.
- A. *Actus reus* (requirement of a criminal act) is the first principle of criminal liability.
- B. Two requirements to prove *actus reus*
  - 1. Bodily movements resulted in criminal act.
  - 2. Bodily movements were voluntary.
- C. Reasoning for the voluntary act requirement
  - 1. Criminal law punishes people.
  - 2. Criminal law can't punish without blame.
  - 3. There is no blame without responsibility.
  - 4. There is no responsibility without a voluntary act (free will).
- D. Status as a criminal act
  - 1. Act is what we do; status is who we are.
  - 2. Status is created in two ways.
    - a. Voluntary act (first use of alcohol or other drug)
    - b. Inherent (race, ethnicity, sex, age)
  - 3. Punishment for status violates U.S. Constitution, Amendment VIII (cruel and unusual punishment), by the same reasoning a voluntary act is required by the principle of *actus reus*.
- E. Failure to act as a criminal act
  - 1. Two types of criminal omissions
    - a. Failure to report (accident, income tax)
    - b. Failure to intervene (call for help or rescue)

2. It's wrong (but not always a crime) to stand by while bad things happen.
    a. Moral and legal duties differ.
    b. Failure to act is a criminal act only when there's a legal duty to act, created by
        (1) Statute
        (2) Contract
        (3) Special relationship
3. Criminal liability exists only when both of the following are true:
    a. There's a legal duty to act.
    b. The legal duty is performed unreasonably.
4. Two approaches to creating and carrying out legal duties toward strangers in trouble
    a. American bystander rule (most states)—no legal duty to rescue or summon help for strangers.
    b. Good Samaritan rule—legal duty to help or summon help for strangers in danger.

F. Possession as a criminal act
1. Possession is a passive state, not a positive act.
2. Legal fiction makes it an act for good policy reasons.
    a. Reduce crime
    b. Many times possession is the result of a voluntary act.
3. Two aspects of possession
    a. Control of items and substances
        (1) Actual (substance or item on the person)
        (2) Constructive (control the stuff but not on the person)
    b. Awareness of control
        (1) Knowing possession (you know you possess the stuff)
        (2) Mere possession (the stuff is physically on you, but you don't know it)
4. Kinds of possession
    a. Control: actual and constructive
    b. Awareness: knowing and mere

CHAPTER SUMMARY

The prosecution is required to prove every element of the crime beyond a reasonable doubt. One basic principle of criminal liability is the requirement of a criminal act. The criminal act is an element of criminal liability that the prosecution has to prove beyond a reasonable doubt.

There are two types of crime based on their elements: crimes of criminal conduct and crimes of criminal conduct causing criminal harms. Crimes of criminal conduct have a mental state and an act triggered by the mental state. The concurrence element requires that the act be caused or triggered by the intent (*mens rea*). Intending to commit a crime is not a crime because it hasn't ripened into a criminal act (*actus reus*). Crimes of criminal conduct causing harm have the additional elements of causation and harm. The act must cause the harm.

The *actus reus* can be a positive act (commission) or omission to act. A criminal act has to be a voluntary bodily movement because we can't blame people for their involuntary acts. Actions refer to what we *do*; status or condition refers to who or what we *are*. Some conditions we're born with; others we produce by our acts. Making disease a crime violates the cruel and unusual punishment clause of the U.S. Constitution, Amendment VIII. It's a criminal act to stand by and do nothing when there's a legal duty to act. A legal duty to act can be imposed by civil or criminal statutes, the common law, a contract or a special relationship.

There are two types of criminal omissions: failure to report and failure to intervene. Criminal omissions create criminal liability only when a legal duty is not reasonably performed.

Possession is a passive state, but it can qualify as a criminal act when properly defined by law. There are a number of aspects or possible elements of possession crimes. First is physical control of an item. Second is awareness of physical control of some item. Third is awareness of the nature of the item (whether it is contraband or not). Actual possession means the item is on your person or within your reach. Constructive possession means the item is under your control but not on your person or within your reach. Things you leave at your home by putting them in your safe (for which you have the combination), are constructively possessed. Mere possession means you have possession of it, and know you have possession, but don't know the nature of the item (that it is contraband). Knowing possession means that you knowingly possess the item and know that the item is contraband. Most states require proof that the possessor knew the item was contraband before a conviction can be obtained.

PRACTICE TEST BANK

Multiple Choice

1. To obtain a conviction, the prosecution must prove every element of the offense beyond _____.
   a. probable cause
   b. a reasonable suspicion
   c. clear and convincing evidence
   d. a reasonable doubt

2. Based on the elements of crime, there are two types of crime: _____.
   a. crimes of criminal conduct and harm
   b. crimes of criminal intent and *mens rea*
   c. crimes of criminal conduct and *actus reus*
   d. overt and covert

3. The essence of the principle of *actus reus* is _____.
   a. intention
   b. act
   c. concurrence
   d. contingency

4. The principle of *mens rea* involves _____.
   a. intent
   b. act
   c. concurrence
   d. harm

5. The requirement of manifest criminality before there is punishment means that _____.
   a. intent alone, without an act, is not a crime
   b. an act alone, without intent, is not a crime
   c. harm alone, without causation, is not a crime
   d. causation alone, without harm, is not a crime

6. To be criminal, an act must be _____.
   a. objective
   b. peremptory
   c. voluntary
   d. the cause of the harm

7. In Powell v. Texas (1968) the Court held that under the Eighth Amendment, an alcoholic _____.
   a. could not be guilty of any crime committed while intoxicated
   b. was not entitled to a constitutional defense of chronic alcoholism
   c. could not be guilty of public intoxication
   d. was not capable of a voluntary act while intoxicated

8. In Robinson v. California (1962), the Court specifically held that under the Eighth Amendment, government could not make it a crime to be _____.
   a. addicted to the use of narcotics
   b. a hypochondriac
   c. a compulsive gambler
   d. a nymphomaniac

9. Under the Eighth Amendment, government cannot punish someone for a _____.
   a. status, disease or condition
   b. a crime that has no *mens rea* element
   c. an act that is not involuntary
   d. a crime that is the result of a psychological compulsion

10. Acts committed during somnambulism or automatism cannot be criminal because the acts _____.
   a. are not reflexive
   b. do not indicate the personality of the offender
   c. are not voluntary
   d. are not spontaneous

11. The term *actus reus* means evil _____.
   a. act
   b. mind
   c. intent
   d. result

12. The element of concurrence means that the _____.
   a. act must cause the intent
   b. harm must flow from intent
   c. intent must cause the act
   d. harm must flow from the act

13. As compared to crimes of criminal conduct, crimes of criminal harm have two additional elements: _____.
   a. concurrence and victimization
   b. causation and harm
   c. conspicuity and damage
   d. contiguity and result

14. The three elements of crimes of criminal conduct are *actus reus*, *mens rea* and _____.
   a. conduct
   b. concurrence
   c. consistence
   d. contagion

15. In terms of *actus reus*, an omission is a _____.
   a. duty
   b. mistake
   c. failure to act
   d. failure to think

16. A legal duty to act is an example of a criminal element called _____.
   a. (attendant) circumstances
   b. *mens rea*
   c. *actus reus*
   d. harm

17. Under the Good Samaritan rule, a person has a legal duty to _____.
   a. report all crimes to the police
   b. investigate crimes they witness
   c. render or summon aid for people in danger
   d. help the poor avoid economic crimes

18. A legal fiction is a legal rule that _____.
   a. assumes the existence of fact that does not exist
   b. distributes the burden of proof
   c. defines the role of the jury in fact-finding
   d. can be overcome by evidence

19. Legally, possession is deemed to be a type of _____.
   a. *mens rea*
   b. harm
   c. act
   d. concurrence

20. A person who is carrying an item in their pocket, purse or backpack is in _____ possession of the container and items therein.
   a. constructive
   b. fictional
   c. derivative
   d. actual

21. To be guilty of possession of contraband, most states require that the prosecution prove that the defendant knew _____.
   a. the quantity of the item possessed
   b. the nature of the item possessed
   c that the item was going to be sold for profit
   d. that the person who gave it to him/her had no right to possess it

22. In contrast to the Good Samaritan rule, the American bystander rule imposes _____.
   a. less duty to help complete strangers
   b. no duty to help one's own children
   c. more duty to assist others
   d. duties only when felonies are involved

23. The two main types of criminal omissions are failure to _____.
   a. report and intervene
   b. act and think
   c. prevent and conclude
   d. act subjectively and objectively

24. A person leaves their heroin at home locked in a safe to which he or she has the combination. The person then goes to the train station. At the train station, this is an example of ____ possession.
   a. fractional
   b. joint
   c. constructive
   d. actual

25. If a person does not know the nature of the item they possess, this is called _____ possession.
   a. fictional
   b. constructive
   c. mere
   d. actual

26. An omission to act is a crime only if there is a _____ duty to act.
   a. fictional
   b. moral
   c. actual
   d. legal

27. The requirement that there be an act element prevents government from punishing people _____.
   a. for bad thoughts only
   b. for their conduct
   c. for the harm they cause
   d. who lack concurrence

28. The requirement that people be punished for acts rather than diseases, conditions or a status grows out of the _____ Amendment.
   a. Fourth
   b. Sixth
   c. Eighth
   d. Ninth

29. The people who watched from their apartments while Kitty Genovese was being murdered in the street and failed to aid her or call the police were not guilty of any crime because they _____.
   a. could not be sure the police would arrive in time
   b. knew the attacker was armed
   c. did not know the identity of the attacker
   d. had no legal duty to aid her or call the police

30. A legal duty can arise from statutes, contracts and _____.
   a. special relationships
   b. manumissions
   c. forfeitures
   d. discretion

True-False

1. The *actus reus* is the mental element of a crime.
   a. true
   b. false

2. The concurrence element means that the mental element must cause the harm.
   a. true
   b. false.

3. The prosecution must prove every element of the crime beyond a reasonable doubt to get a conviction.
   a. true
   b. false

4. The *mens rea* is the harm element of a crime.
   a. true
   b. false

5. To be guilty of a criminal harm offense, the defendant must have caused the harm.
   a. true
   b. false

6. Crimes of criminal conduct have no concurrence element.
   a. true
   b. false

7. The term *actus reus* means evil act.
   a. true
   b. false

8. Under the Model Penal Code to be guilty of an omission to act, the act must be one that the defendant was physically capable of performing.
   a. true
   b. false

9. Somnambulism is sleepwalking.
   a. true
   b. false

10. A reflex or spasm is a voluntary act.
    a. true
    b. false

11. In Robinson v. California the U.S. Supreme Court held that governments may omit the *actus reus* element when defining crimes.
    a. true
    b. false

12. In Powell v. Texas, the Court held that government cannot punish an alcoholic for any crimes committed while intoxicated.
    a. true
    b. false

13. Government cannot punish a person solely for their status, condition or disease.
    a. true
    b. false

14. A failure to act is termed an omission.
    a. true
    b. false

15. A failure to act can be a crime only if there is a legal duty to do the act.
    a. true
    b. false

16. All moral duties are also legal duties.
    a. true
    b. false

17. The Good Samaritan rule imposes more duties to assist than does the American bystander rule.
    a. true
    b. false

18. A contract cannot create a legal duty to act.
    a. true
    b. false

19. Most states punish mere possession of contraband.
    a. true
    b. false

20. If an item is in a defendant's pocket, he is in actual possession of that item.
    a. true
    b. false

21. The concept of manifest criminality requires that the defendant's acts cause harm.
    a. true
    b. false

22. A legal fiction is something that is always true.
   a. true
   b. false

23. The mere presence of the accused on shared premises where contraband is found is, by itself, not enough to prove ownership or possession.
   a. true
   b. false

24. Knowing possession means that the person knows such possession is illegal.
   a. true
   b. false

25. The ban on cruel and unusual punishment is found in the Eighth Amendment.
   a. true
   b. false

Fill in the blank

1. Another term for sleepwalking is ____________.

2. The ________________ is the act element of the crime

3. The ________________ is the mental element of the crime.

4. The _____________ element requires that the mental element cause the act.

5. If a person commits an act during a state of automatism, the act is probably not a crime because the act is not ______________.

6. The prosecution must prove every _____________ of the crime beyond a reasonable doubt.

7. A failure to act is called a/n _____________.

8. A failure to act is not a crime unless there is a _____________ duty to do the act.

9. Persons have a broad duty to assist others under the ________________ rule.

10. Under the ________________ rule, people have little or no duty to assist strangers in peril.

11. In _____________, the Court held that a person could not be punished for being a drug addict.

12. Possessing some item but not knowing the nature of the item is called ____________ possession.

13. Although it may be a legal fiction, possession is deemed to be a form of ____________.

14. Before it can be a crime, most states require that possession be ____________ rather than just mere possession.

15. If a person leaves an item at home and goes elsewhere, they can still be in ____________ possession of that item.

Essay

1. Explain why only voluntary acts are crimes. Be sure to provide examples.

2. Compare and contrast actual and constructive possession. Provide examples of each.

3. Compare and contrast knowing and mere possession. Provide examples of each.

4. Under what circumstances can an omission to act be deemed the *actus reus* of a crime? Be sure to provide examples.

5. Compare and contrast the Good Samaritan doctrine and the American bystander rule.

CHAPTER 3 ANSWER KEY

Multiple Choice

1—d (55) 2—a (56) 3—b (55) 4—a (55) 5—a (58)

6—c (58) 7—b (65) 8—a (63) 9—a (63) 10—c (59)

11—a (55) 12—c (55) 13—b (56) 14—b (56) 15—c (67)

16—a (67) 17—c (68) 18—a (77) 19—c (77) 20—d (78)

21—b (78) 22—a (68) 23—a (68) 24—c (78) 25—c (78)

26—d (67) 27—a (58) 28—c (63) 29—d (75) 30—a (67)

True-False

1—T (55) 2—F (55) 3—T (55) 4—F (55) 5—T (56)

6—F (56) 7—T (55) 8—T (58) 9 T (59) 10—F (63)

11—F (63) 12—F (65) 13—T (63(14—T (65) 15—T (67)

16—F (67) 17—T (67) 18—F (67) 19—F (78) 20—T (78)

21—F (58) 22—F (77) 23—T (82_ 24—F (78) 25—T (63)

Fill in the blank

1—somnambulism (59) 2—*actus reus* (55) 3—*mens rea* (55) 4—concurrence (55)

5—voluntary (58) 6—element (55) 7—omission (67) 8—legal (67)

9—Good Samaritan (68) 10—American bystander (68) 11—Robinson v. California (63)

12—mere (78) 13—*actus reus* (55) 14—knowing (78) 15—constructive (78)

Chapter 4 The General Principles of Criminal Liability: Mens Rea, Concurrence and Causation

LEARNING OBJECTIVES

After studying this chapte,r students will

1. understand the concept of *mens rea,* or the mental element of crime.
2. be familiar with the major types of *mens rea.*
3. understand how *mens rea* can be proven.
4. know the definition of a strict liability crime.
5. be familiar with arguments for and against strict liability crimes.
6. know that the *mens rea* must cause the act for there to be criminal liability (concurrence).
7. understand the concepts of factual (but for) and legal (proximate) cause.
8. understand how intervening cause can affect criminal liability.

KEY TERMS AND CONCEPTS

Mens rea—the mental or intent element of a crime; p. 87
Culpability—mental blameworthiness or intent; p. 87
Blameworthiness—responsible and deserving of punishment; p. 87
Circumstantial evidence—indirect evidence of a fact; p. 88
General intent—intent to do the act; p. 88
Specific intent—*mens rea* element that applies to something other than the act; p. 88
Transferred intent—doctrine transferring defendant's intent from intended to actual victim; p. 88
Constructive intent—rule making person responsible for harm greater than what they intended; p. 8
Purpose—most blameworthy of the Model Penal Code forms of *mens rea*; means conscious desire or purpose; p. 90
Knowledge—Model Penal Code form of intent involving awareness of potential harm; p. 94
Recklessness—Model Penal Code form of intent involving consciousness of serious risk but taking risk; p. 97
Negligence—failure to behave as a reasonable person would have under the same circumstances; p. 98
Intervening cause—factor after defendant's act contributing to causation of the harm.
Proximate or legal cause—issue of fairness of making defendant liable for the resulting harm; p. 106
Strict liability offense—one that has no *mens rea* element; p. 100
But for test—harm would not have occurred except for defendant's acts; p. 106

CHAPTER OUTLINE

I. *Mens rea* is the mental element of a crime that the prosecution must prove beyond a reasonable doubt.
   - A. Serious crimes require both a criminal act (*actus reus*) and criminal intent (*mens rea*).
   - B. Proof of *mens rea*
     - 1. We can't see intent or measure it directly.
     - 2. We infer intent from actors' actions (circumstantial evidence).
   - C. Four kinds of *mens rea* (criminal intent or blameworthy state of mind)
     - 1. *Mens rea* consists of four states of mind with different levels of culpability.
     - 2. The four levels of culpability are:
       - a. Purpose (or intentionally)—acting on purpose and/or with the conscious object of causing harm.
       - b. Knowledge—acting knowingly but without the conscious purpose or object of causing harm.
       - c. Recklessness—acting with a conscious creation of a high risk of harm.
       - d. Negligence (or criminal negligence)—acting with an unconscious creation of a high risk of harm.
   - D. Strict liability offenses don't require culpability (i.e., *mens rea*).
     - 1. Justifications for strict liability
       - a. The offenses are a danger to public health, safety, and morals.
       - b. Penalties are limited to fines as the only punishment.
     - 2. Criticisms of strict liability
       - a. It violates the basic idea of punishment for culpability.
       - b. It could be expanded to include more serious crimes.

II. The principle of concurrence states the required relationship between intent and act.
   - A. *Mens rea* triggers the criminal act.
   - B. Criminal conduct causes the criminal harm.

III. The principle of causation states the required relationship between act and harm.
   - A. Applies only to crimes of criminal conduct causing criminal harm.
   - B. Two kinds of causation
     - 1. Factual ("but for" or "except for") cause
       - a. Is an empirical question of fact
       - b. "Except for" or "but for" an act by the defendant that triggered a chain of events, would this criminal harm have occurred?
       - c. A necessary but not sufficient cause for proving causation

2. Legal (proximate) cause
    a. Based on a subjective question of fairness: Should the defendant be blamed and punished for this injury or death?
    b. Two types of intervening acts in the chain between the triggering act of the defendant and the criminal harm
        (1) Coincidental intervening acts break the causal chain unless they're predictable or foreseeable.
        (2) Responsive intervening acts only break the causal chain if
            a) They're abnormal, or,
            b) They're not predicable or foreseeable.

CHAPTER SUMMARY

Most crimes have a *mens rea* or mental element that must be proven by the prosecution beyond a reasonable doubt. The basic idea is that it is not fair to punish someone unless they had some form of mental fault or blameworthiness.

The mental element can apply to or modify other elements of a crime and thus a crime can have more than one mental element. For instance, the *mens rea* can apply to the act, the harm or the circumstances.

General intent means intent to do the criminal act. Specific intent means an intent that applies to any other element of the crime other than the criminal act. Transferred intent is a doctrine that transfers the criminal's intent from the intended victim to the victim the criminal actually hurt.

There are many different types of intent or culpability in various jurisdictions. Many states follow the Model Penal Code approach of having only four types of culpability or *mens rea*. The first is purpose. This means it was the actor's conscious object. Knowing means that the actor knew something was likely to happen or occur. Recklessness means that the person was aware of a serious risk but went ahead and took that risk anyway, even though an objectively reasonable person would not have taken that risk. Negligence means the actor did not conform to the external, objective standard of what a reasonable person would have known or done in the same circumstances. Purpose and knowing are subjective mental states. Recklessness is both objective and subjective. Negligence is a totally objective standard.

A few crimes do not have a *mens rea* element. These are called strict liability crimes. These crimes are controversial because they can punish persons who had no mental fault. A person could be punished for an accident. On the other hand, it is argued that certain types of crimes involve such important governmental interests and would be too difficult to enforce if a *mens rea* element was required. Strict liability crimes are always minor crimes that are rarely, if ever, punished by imprisonment.

If a crime has a harm or result element, the prosecution must prove that the defendant caused the harm beyond a reasonable doubt. The prosecution must prove that the defendant's acts were both (1) the cause in fact (but for cause) and (2) the proximate or legal cause. Cause in fact is an empirical or factual issue. Proximate or legal cause involves the question of whether it is fair or just to make the defendant responsible for a harm that occurred in an unusual fashion. For instance, sometimes a defendant will do an act and start a chain of events in motion, but some other events will occur after the defendant's act and contribute to causation of the harm. In general, if this intervening cause was normal and foreseeable, the defendant will not be relieved of liability for the harm.

PRACTICE TEST BANK

Multiple Choice

1. The mental element of a crime is called the _____.
   a. *actus reus*
   b. *mens rea*
   c. harm
   d. concurrence

2. In the absence of a confession, intent must generally be proven by _____ evidence.
   a. peremptory
   b. exclusive
   c. referential
   d. circumstantial

3. General intent is the intent to _____.
   a. do a criminal act
   b. cause a result
   c. cause the circumstances
   d. have the *mens rea*

4. The doctrine of transferred intent applies when _____.
   a. an unintended victim or property is harmed by the defendant
   b. the statute is a strict liability one
   c. there is no causal element
   d. the concurrence element is missing

5 A *mens rea* requirement that applies to anything other than the *actus reus* is called ________ intent.
   a. strict
   b. specific
   c. transferred
   d. general

6. The objective reasonable person standard is used in the definition of _____.
   a. negligence
   b. purposely
   c. knowingly
   d. transferred intent

7. The strongest objection to strict liability laws is that _____.
   a. they result in the punishment of people who are not blameworthy
   b. long periods of imprisonment are authorized for such offenses
   c. there is no strong public interest in preventing these crimes
   d. conviction of such offenses carries a heavy stigma equivalent to burglary or robbery

8. The actor intends (or it is his purpose) to kill Ms. A. He shoots at Ms. A and misses but kills Ms. B instead. The actor's argument that he is not guilty of murder because he did not intend to kill Ms. B will be defeated by the doctrine of _____.
   a. circumstantial evidence
   b. transferred intent
   c. general intent
   d. concurrence

9. A defendant is criminally responsible for harm if the defendant's conduct was the _____.
   a. cause in fact and proximate cause
   b. but for cause of the harm
   c. natural result of the conduct
   d. intervening cause

10. *Mens rea* elements _____.
   a. apply only to the act element
   b. apply only to the harm element
   c. can apply to other *mens rea* elements
   d. can apply to any other element except *mens rea*

11. Which of the following is not a type of culpability in the Model Penal Code?
   a. purpose
   b. knowledge
   c. intention
   d. negligence

12. If it is not the defendant's conscious object to cause the harm but he is aware that the harm will occur, the defendant is said to have the *mens rea* termed _____.
   a. knowledge
   b. consciousness.
   c. awareness
   d. complicity

13. Conscious risk creation is referred to as _____.
   a. purpose
   b. negligence
   c. recklessness
   d. perspicacity

14. If an actor does not behave like an objectively reasonable person would have under the same circumstances, the actor is _____.
   a. reckless
   b. feckless
   c. wanton
   d. negligent

15. Which of the following types of culpability is both objective and subjective?
   a. negligent
   b. reckless
   c. knowing
   d. purpose

16. A crime that lacks a _____ element is called a strict liability crime.
   a. vicarious
   b. indirect
   c. covert
   d. strict

17. Factual cause is also referred to as a ______ cause.
   a. legal
   b. proximate
   c. but for
   d. distal

18. An event that occurs between the defendant's act and the harm and has a causal connection to the harm is called an _____ act or cause.
   a. intervening
   b. concurrent
   c. consecutive
   d. contingent

19. The prosecution must prove that the defendant caused the harm _____.
   a. by a preponderance of the evidence
   b. beyond a moral certainty
   c. by clear and convincing evidence
   d. beyond a reasonable doubt

20. One definition of the term concurrence requires that the criminal intent _____.
   a. cause the act
   b. cause the harm
   c. cause the *mens rea*
   d. be the proximate cause of the circumstances

21. The U.S. Supreme Court has ruled that the U.S. Constitution requires that all crimes have a/n _____ element.
    a. *mens rea*
    b. act
    c. transferred intent
    d. harm

22. In the Model Penal Code, the most blameworthy state of mind is _____.
    a. recklessness
    b. negligent
    c. purpose
    d. intention

23. An accidental injury can be a crime if the criminal statute is of the _____ type.
    a. strict liability
    b. capital
    c. vicarious liability
    d. mendacious

24. But for causation can also be referred to as _____ for causation.
    a. except
    b. in lieu
    c. and
    d. contingent

25. Legal or proximate cause issues involve the _____.
    a. empirical connection between the act and harm
    b. but for test
    c. except for test
    d. justice of making the defendant responsible for this harm

26. If a responsive intervening act is normal and foreseeable, the defendant _____.
    a. is not responsible for the harm
    b. is responsible only for negligent offenses
    c. is responsible only for reckless harms
    d. is responsible for the harm

27. A statute which makes it a crime to select the victim because of the defendant's hostility toward their race, ethnic group, religious group, etc., is called a ____ crime.
    a. prejudice
    b. discrimination
    c. animus
    d. hate

28. A criminal statute is more likely to have more than one ____ element than it is to have more than one element of any other kind.
   a. intent
   b. act
   c. cause
   d. concurrence

29. U.S. Supreme Court Justice Oliver Wendell Holmes statement that even a dog can distinguish between a kick and being stumbled over, highlights the importance of the _____ element of crimes.
   a. harm
   b. result
   c. concurrence
   d. intent

30. Being aware of a serious risk but going ahead and taking it anyway is the form of intent termed _____.
   a. negligence
   b. recklessness
   c. knowledge
   d. purpose

True-False

1. In the absence of a confession, *mens rea* is usually proven by circumstantial evidence.
   a. true
   b. false

2. Different kinds of intent indicate different levels of blameworthiness.
   a. true
   b. false

3. Specific intent is intent to do the criminal act.
   a. true
   b. false

4. The four levels of culpability or intent in the Model Penal Code are purpose, knowledge, recklessness and negligence.
   a. true
   b. false

5. Negligence is the most blameworthy form of intent.
   a. true
   b. false

6. Recklessness requires awareness of substantial and unjustifiable risks.
   a. true
   b. false

7. Negligence has both an objective and subjective component.
   a. true
   b. false

8. Strict liability crimes have no *actus reus* element.
   a. true
   b. false

9. In strict liability crimes, accidental injury can be criminal.
   a. true
   b. false

10. Proving criminal causation requires proving both factual and legal cause.
    a. true
    b. false

11. Intervening causes can never be proximate causes.
    a. true
    b. false

12. Specific intent is intent that is transferred to another victim.
    a. true
    b. false

13. The most blameworthy state of mind in the Model Penal Code is purpose.
    a. true
    b. false

14. Negligence involves conscious risk creation.
    a. true
    b. false

15. The issue of factual cause involves the but for test.
    a. true
    b. false

16. Negligence is a totally objective standard.
    a. true
    b. false

17. Questions of fairness and justice figure into the factual cause determination.
    a. true
    b. false

18. Factual cause is an empirical question.
    a. true
    b. false

19. A normal, foreseeable, responsive intervening act will not prevent criminal liability for a crime.
    a. true
    b. false

20. An abnormal and unforeseeable intervening cause will generally not relieve the defendant of liability for causing the harm.
    a. true
    b. false

21. An earthquake could be an intervening cause.
    a. true
    b. false

22. Strict liability crimes always violate due process
    a. true
    b. false

23. Premeditation, wickedly and designedly are all example of *mens rea*.
    a. true
    b. false

24. A hate crime is one motivated by a desire for revenge against this particular victim.
    a. true
    b. false

25. The burden of proof on the causation issue is on the defendant.
    a. true
    b. false

<u>Fill in the blank</u>

1. The except for test is better known as the _______________ test.

2. Fairness and justice come into play in the legal or _______________ test of causation.

3. The form of intent involving having a conscious object is _______________.

4. Negligence is a totally ______________ standard.

5. ______________ involves conscious risk creation.

6. __________________ is intent to do the criminal act.

7. The mental element of the crime is called the ________________.

8. ______________ evidence proves a fact indirectly or by inference.

9. _________________ is intent that applies to elements other than the act.

10. The doctrine of _________________ shifts the intent from the intended victim to the actual victim.

11. A ______________ crime is one motivated by dislike of the victim's race, ethnicity, etc.

12. A crime without an intent element is called a _________________ crime.

13. The most blameworthy form of intent in the Model Penal Code is ______________.

14. The least blameworthy form of intent in the Model Penal Code is ______________.

15. Proximate cause is also referred to as ________________.

Essay

1. Compare and contrast specific and general intent. Be sure to provide examples.

2. Define and discuss strict liability crimes. What is the justification for such crimes? Be sure to provide examples.

3. What does the criminal law require in the way of a relationship between the act and intent? Why is this relationship important? Be sure to provide examples.

4. Compare and contrast transferred and constructive intent. Be sure to provide examples.

5. List and define the four types of *mens rea* found in the Model Penal Code. Define each and give an example.

CHAPTER 4 ANSWER KEY

Multiple Choice

1—b (87)	2—d (88)	3—a (88)	4—a (88)	5—b (88)
6—a (98)	7—a (101)	8—b (88)	9—a (106)	10—d (88)
11—c (89)	12—a (94)	13—c (97)	14—d (98)	15—b (98)
16—d (100)	17—c (104)	18—a (107)	19—d (105)	20—a (105)
21—b (101)	22—c (90)	23—a (100)	24—a (105)	25—d (106)
26—d (107)	27—d (92)	28—a (87)	29—d (87)	30—b (89)

True-False

1—T (88)	2—T (87)	3—F (88)	4—T (89)	5—F (90)
6—T (97)	7—F (98)	8—F (100)	9—T (100)	10—T (105)
11—F (107)	12—F (88)	13—T (90)	14—F (97)	15—T (106)
16—T (98)	17—F (106)	18—T (106)	19—T (107)	20—F (107)
21—T (107)	22—F (101)	23—T (87)	24—F (92)	25—F (105)

Fill in the blank

1—but for (106)	2—proximate (101)	3—purpose (90)	4—objective (98)
5—Recklessness (97)	6—general intent (88)	7—*mens rea* (87)	8—circumstantial (88)
9—specific intent (88)	10—transferred intent (88)	11—hate (92)	12—strict liability (100)
13—purpose (90)	14—negligence (98)	15—legal cause (106)	

Chapter 5 Parties to Crime and Vicarious Liability

LEARNING OBJECTIVES

After studying this chapter, students will

1. understand the doctrines of complicity or parties to crime.
2. be familiar with the common law approach to complicity.
3. understand the current distinction between accomplices and accessories.
4. be familiar with the crime of conspiracy.
5. know the Pinkerton rule.
6. understand the *mens rea* and *actus reus* of accomplice liability.
7. be familiar with accessory-after-the-fact statutes.
8. understand now vicarious liability and strict liability apply against corporate crime.
9. understand how vicarious liability can apply against individuals.
10. be familiar with the issues surrounding vicarious liability of parents.

KEY TERMS AND CONCEPTS

Parties to crime—persons who are liable for the acts of another; p. 115
Complicity—makes persons liable for the acts of another; 115
Vicarious liability—liability for the acts of another because of relationship to the other; p. 115
Doctrine of complicity—rules that establish when one is liable for the acts of another; p. 115
Doctrine of vicarious liability—rules establishing when one is vicariously liable for acts of others; p. 115
Principals in the first degree—at common law, person who actually committed crime; p. 116
Principals in the second degree—at common law, persons involved in crime who were present at the scene of crime; p. 116
Accessories before the fact—at common law, persons who assisted before crime committed; p. 116
Accessories after the fact—at common law, persons who assisted after crime completed; p. 116
Accomplices—participants before and/or during the crime; p. 116
Accessories—participants after the crime is completed; p. 116
Conspiracy—agreement to commit a crime; p. 116
Pinkerton rule—conspirators can be convicted of both conspiracy and the crime committed; p. 116
Accomplice *actus reus*—acts necessary to become an accomplice (e.g., aiding); p. 117
Mere presence rule—presence at scene of crime alone does not make one an accomplice; p. 117
Prima facie—adequate to establish a presumption (of guilty); p. 136
Parental responsibility laws—laws making parents responsible for acts of offspring; p. 139

CHAPTER OUTLINE

I. There are two types of liability for someone else's criminal acts:
  A. Parties to crime (complicity) establish when you can be held liable for crimes of another.
  B. Vicarious liability establishes which types of relationships can create criminal liability.

II. Parties to crime are responsible for the crime.
  A. There were four types of parties to crime at common law:
    1. Principals in the first degree actually commit the crime.
    2. Principles in the second degree are present when the crimes are committed.
    3. Accessories before the fact
      a. Help before the crime is committed.
      b. Are not present when the crime is committed.
    4. Accessories after the fact help after the crime is committed.
  B. Participation before and during crime (accomplices)
    1. Are prosecuted for committing the crime itself (helping a murderer is murder).
    2. Accomplice *actus reus*
      a. Core idea—accomplice took some positive act to help commit a crime.
      b. Words can be accomplice *actus reus*.
      c. Presence at the crime scene isn't enough unless there's a duty (parent to minor child).
      d. Actions after the crime can be relevant to prove *actus reus*.
    3. Accomplice *mens rea*
      a. Purposely clearly qualifies.
      b. Jurisdictions vary and sometimes are confused as to whether knowledge, recklessness, or negligence qualify.
  C. Participation after the commission of a crime (accessory)
    1. Is a separate lesser offense than accomplice liability.
    2. Elements of accessory after the fact
      a. Accessory personally helped the person who committed the felony (*actus reus* element).
      b. Accessory knew a felony was committed (*mens rea* element).
      c. Accessory helped for the purpose of hindering prosecution (*mens rea* element).
      d. Someone other than the accessory actually committed a felony (circumstance element).

III. Vicarious liability makes one liable for the acts of another because of a relationship.
  A. Vicarious liability bases liability on a relationship between a person who commits the crime and another.
  B. Corporate vicarious liability
    1. Pinpointing responsibility is difficult because of the complexity of organizations and the number of people making decisions.
    2. Constitutional and policy issues
      a. Due process issues

(1) Liability is based on relationship and not acts and/or intent.

(2) Fairness to shareholders, who usually pay the fines.

b. Policy question—deterrence?

C. Individual vicarious liability

1. Traffic violation

a. Difficulty proving who parked the vehicle.

b. *Prima facie* case—presumes driver was the operator and is responsible.

2. Parental responsibility—parents responsible for acts of children.

CHAPTER SUMMARY

A person can be criminally liable for the criminal acts of another. The doctrine of complicity (parties to crime) establishes when you can be held criminally liable for someone else's crimes. The doctrine of vicarious liability establishes what types of relationships can make you liable for someone else's crimes.

The common law on complicity was complex. A principal in the first degree was the person who actually committed the crime. Principals in the second degree were those who were present at the scene of the crime and aided the principal in the first degree. Such aid could take the form of being a lookout or driving the getaway car. Accessories before the fact were those who were involved in the crime before it was committed and were not present when it was committed. An example would be a person who provides safe-cracking tools for the safecracker. Finally, an accessory after the fact is one whose only aid comes after the crime was completed.

Today, the law has been simplified. Under the current approach, participants before and during the commission of crimes are guilty of the crime itself. These persons are liable as accomplices. Participants after the commission of crimes are guilty of a separate, less serious offense.

Persons in a conspiracy to commit a crime can also be liable for both the conspiracy and the crimes of other conspirators. This flows from the Pinkerton rule.

The essence of accomplice *actus reus* is that the accomplice took some positive action to aid or assist in the commission of a crime actually committed by another. The *mens rea* of complicity varies; depending on the jurisdiction. It may be purpose, knowledge, recklessness, or negligence. The core idea of accessory liability is that it's not as blameworthy to help someone else escape prosecution as it is to participate in the crime itself.

Mens rea in business crimes is hard to prove because of the size and complexity of organizations and decision-making. Legislatures attempt to overcome this by creating strict liability crimes (eliminating any *mens rea*) and/or creating vicarious liability. Vicarious liability raises due process constitutional issues and policy questions about its effectiveness.

Individual vicarious liability involves making an individual responsible for the acts of other individuals: for instance, making owners of cars vicariously liable for operators' parking tickets. The liability is created because of the owner-operator relationship.

Vicarious liability of parents based on the parent-child relationship grew out of public fear, frustration, and anger over juvenile crime. There is little case law on such statutes and some have been held unconstitutional.

PRACTICE TEST BANK

Multiple Choice

1. The _____ rule or principle states that everyone who is involved in a crime, whether before, during or after, may be responsible for that crime.
   a. vicarious liability
   b. complicity
   c. Pinkerton
   d. Wharton

2. Mr. A robs the bank. Mr. B waits outside with the getaway car. Under the common law, with regard to the bank robbery, Mr. B is a _____.
   a. principal in the first degree
   b. accessory after the fact
   c. accessory before the fact
   d. principal in the second degree

3. Mr. A commits a burglary. A few days before, he got the burglary tools from Mr. B. Mr. B has not other involvement in the burglary. Under the common law approach, Mr. B is a _____.
   a. accessory before the fact
   b. accessory after the fact
   c. principle in the third degree
   d. principal in the second degree

4. An agreement between two or more persons to commit a crime is a/an _____.
   a. solicitation
   b. conspiracy
   c. complicity crime
   d. vicarious liability offense

5. The current approach to complicity _____.
   a. maintains most of the common law distinctions
   b. eliminates the principle and accessory classifications of the common law
   c. retains the common law terminology of accessories before the fact
   d. retains the common law terminology of principal in the second degree

6. Accomplice liability _____.
   a. requires *actus reus* but not *mens rea*
   b. requires *mens rea* but no *actus reus*
   c. requires both *actus reus* and *mens rea*
   d. is a strict liability offense

7. The Pinkerton rule is applicable only to _____.
   a. accomplices
   b. the doctrine of complicity
   c. conspiracies
   d. accessories

8. Vicarious liability arises most frequently in employment or _____ relationships.
   a. personal
   b. producer-consumer
   c. family
   d. business

9. To convict a person of being an accessory after the fact, the government must show that _____.
   a. the person intended to aid the criminal after the crime
   b. there was a conspiracy to aid after the crime entered into before the crime
   c. the Pinkerton rule applies
   d. the person provided aid to a person whom he knew had committed a misdemeanor

10. In general, merely being present at the scene of a crime _____.
   a. is sufficient to create accomplice liable
   b. is not sufficient to create accomplice liability
   c. is the *actus reus* of accomplice liability
   d. creates a presumption that there was a conspiracy to commit the crime

11. To assist in proving corporate liability, legislatures and prosecutor typically rely on two doctrines, _____.
   a. conspiracy and complicity
   b. strict and complicity liability
   c. principal and accessory liability
   d. strict and vicarious liability

12. In State v. Akers, the New Hampshire appellate court overturned the parents' vicarious liability conviction for acts of their children because the law _____.
   a. violated equal protection because it applied only to parents
   b. violated substantive due process by punishing parenthood
   c. was a bill of attainder
   d. was overbroad

13. Mere presence of the actor at the scene of a crime may create accomplice liability _____.
    a. if the actor has a duty to prevent the crime and fails to prevent or attempt to prevent it
    b. if the actor secretly hopes the crime will be completed
    c. the actor knows the victim but does not intervene
    d. the actor knows the criminal but does not intervene

14. A _____ is an agreement between two or more people to commit a crime.
    a. contract
    b. confluence
    c. conspiracy
    d. concurrence

15. The rule that the conspiracy to commit a crime and the crimes committed pursuant to the conspiracy are separate offenses is called the _____ rule.
    a. Wharton
    b. Peoni
    c. Brady
    d. Pinkerton

16. The _____ of accomplice liability is frequently phrased in terms of aiding, abetting or assisting another who commits a crime.
    a. *mens rea*
    b. *actus reus*
    c. circumstances
    d. concurrence

17. According to the U.S. Supreme Court in Bailey v. U.S. (1969), flight from the scene of a crime _____.
    a. by itself proves accomplice liability
    b. by itself proves guilty of the crime
    c. is not evidence of accomplice liability
    d. by itself cannot prove accomplice liability

18. In State v. Ulvinen (1983), the Minnesota appellate court held that _____ alone could not prove accomplice liability for murder.
    a. being related to the victim
    b. living in the same household as the victim
    c. passive approval of the crime
    d. refusing to cooperate with the police

19. The rule of the Peoni case requires that the accomplice not only intent to aid the offender, and know of the crime to be committed, but that the accomplice also intent or desire that _____.

a. the crime be committed
b. there be a conspiracy
c. the actual offender not be caught
d. the accomplice not be caught

20. The early decisions on accomplice liability held that the only *mens rea* required for accomplice liability was intent _____.

a. to aid the offender knowing a crime would be committed
b. to form a conspiracy
c. that the offender commit the crime
d. to benefit from the crime committed

21. Crimes involving being an accessory after the fact typically have _____ *mens rea* element(s).

a. one
b. two
c. three
d. four

22. Most accessory after the fact criminal statutes contain _____ circumstance element(s).

a. no
b. one
c. two
d. three

23. Unlike accomplice liability, vicarious liability does not require that the person being held vicariously liable _____.

a. participate in the crime
b. be aware of the circumstances
c. be involved in a conspiracy
d. not be involved in a conspiracy

24. Strict liability crimes have no _____.

a. *actus reus*
b. voluntary act element
c. legality requirement
d. *mens rea* element

25. Vicarious liability is based on _____.

a. benefiting from the crime
b. being involved in the crime
c. relationships
d. personal *actus reus* and *mens rea*

26. Vicarious liability of individuals usually involves _____.
   a. homicides
   b. traffic tickets
   c. felonies
   d. conspiracies

27. _____ laws make parents liable for the crimes of their children if the parents fail to supervise and control their children.
   a. Parental responsibility
   b. Vicarious parental liability
   c. Conspiracy
   d. Parental combination

28. Corporate liability is always a form of _____ liability.
   a. co-conspirator
   b. accomplice
   c. accessory
   d. vicarious

29. If the owner of a vehicle is *prima facie* responsible for parking tickets issued on that vehicle, this means that the owner _____.
   a. is guilty of conspiracy regarding the violation
   b. is presumed responsible for the violation
   c. is an accomplice to the violation
   d. is an accessory to the violation

30. Many vicarious liability statutes _____.
   a. violate due process, the presumption of innocence, and the Eighth Amendment
   c. are felony statutes
   d. are also strict liability statutes
   e. require that the prosecution prove a conspiracy

True-False

1. Complicity creates liability because of a relationship with the offender.
   a. true
   b. false

2. Vicarious liability hinges on providing aid or assistance to an offender.
   a. true
   b. false

3. At common law, the person who actually committed the crime is the principal in the first degree.
   a. true
   b. false

4. A co-conspirator could be an accessory before the fact.
   a. true
   b. false

5. The Pinkerton rule states that accomplices are liable for all crimes committed by the persons they aid.
   a. true
   b. false

6. The doctrine of complicity establishes when one person can be criminally liable for the acts of another.
   a. true
   b. false

7. At common law, a person who knowingly harbored a felony fugitive to prevent the felon's capture would be an accessory after the fact.
   a. true
   b. false

8. At common law, a person who acted as a lookout for another criminal would be a principal in the third degree.
   a. true
   b. false

9. A person who aids, abets or assists another in committing a crime is an accomplice to that crime.
   a. true
   b. false

10. Flight from the scene of a crime is enough evidence to convict of a crime or being an accomplice.
    a. true
    b. false

11. Mere presence at the scene of a crime is, all by itself, not enough to convict one of being an accomplice to that crime.
    a. true
    b. false

12. Barring some duty to the victim, passive approval of a crime is, by itself, enough to warrant conviction as an accomplice.
    a. true
    b. false

13. Early court decisions on accomplice liability did not require proof of intent to facilitate the crime, only proof of intent to aid the criminal.
    a. true
    b. false

14. The minority rule is that in addition to general intent, accomplice liability also requires intent that the crime be committed.
    a. true
    b. false

15. A person cannot be held liable as an accomplice for negligent or reckless acts.
    a. true
    b. false

16. Most accessory-after-the-fact statutes require that the defendant know the person aided committed a felony.
    a. true
    b. false

17. Accessory and accomplice liability can be established by circumstantial evidence.
    a. true
    b. false

18. A strict liability offense has no *actus reus* element.
    a. true
    b. false

19. Corporations cannot be vicariously liable for the acts of their employees.
    a. true
    b. false

20. Many offenses related to businesses and corporations are both strict and vicarious liability.
    a. true
    b. false

21. A person can be vicariously liable even though they personally did no act and had no criminal intent.
    a. true
    b. false

22. A person who is *prima facie* responsible is presumed responsible.
    a. true
    b. false

23. Parental responsibility laws make parents liable if their children commit a crime because the parents failed to supervise or control their children.
    a. true
    b. false

24. Every law imposing vicarious criminal liability on parents for the acts of their children has been found to be constitutional.
    a. true
    b. false

25. Statutes that impose both strict and vicarious liability always violate due process.
    a. true
    b. false

<u>Fill in the blank</u>

1. Laws making parents liable for acts of offspring because of failure to control or supervise are called ____________________ laws.

2. At common law, persons who protected or harbored the felon after the felony was completed were called accessories after the _______________.

3. The doctrine of ______________ sometimes makes persons liable for the acts of others.

4. ____________________ makes one liable for the acts of another because of the relationship to the other.

5. At common law, person who actually committed crime was termed a _______________ in the first degree.

6. At common law, persons who assisted the criminal before crime was committed were called _____________________.

7. At common law, persons involved in crime who were present at the scene of crime were termed __________________________________.

8. In most jurisdictions today, participants before and/or during the crime are called _______________.

9. An agreement to commit a crime is called a _______________.

10. Under the _______________ rule, conspirators can be convicted of both conspiracy and the crime committed.

11. The term ________________means adequate to establish a presumption of guilt.

12. A crime without a *mens rea* element is called a ____________________ crime.

13. A well established rule states that ____________________ at the scene of a crime is, alone, not enough to justify conviction as an accomplice.

14. Aiding, abetting, assisting, etc. are the *actus reus* of ________________.

15. In many modern codes, a person who assists a criminal after the crime is called a(n) ________________.

<u>Essay</u>

1. Discuss the four parties to a crime under the Common Law. Provide an example of each.

2. Describe, define, compare and contrast the mere presence and Pinkerton rules.

3. Describe, define, compare and contrast accomplice and vicarious liability. Be sure to provide examples.

4. Why does government find it necessary to use vicarious liability and strict liability crimes to fight corporate crime? Be sure to provide examples.

5. What are the four elements of most accessory-after-the-fact statutes? Provide an example of each element.

CHAPTER 5 ANSWER KEY

Multiple Choice

1—b (115) 2—d (116) 3—a (116) 4—b (116) 5—b (116)

6—c (117) 7—c (116) 8—d (129) 9—a (125) 10—b (117)

11—d (129) 12—b (141) 13—a (117) 14—c (116) 15—d (116)

16—b (117) 17—d (117) 18—c (119) 19—a (122) 20—a (121)

21—b (125) 22—b (125) 23—a (129) 24—d (129) 25—c (130)

26—b (136) 27—a (139) 28—d (129) 29—b (136) 30—d (129)

True-False

1—F (115) 2—F (115) 3—T (116) 4—T (116) 5—F (116)

6—T (115) 7—T (166) 8—F (116) 9—T (117) 10—F (117)

11—T (117) 12—F (119) 13—T (128) 14—T (122) 15—F (124)

16—T (123) 17—T (128) 18—F (129) 19—F (129) 20—T (129)

21—T (130) 22—T (136) 23—T (139) 24—F (141) 25—F (129)

Fill in the blank

1—parental responsibility (139) 2—fact (116) 3—complicity (115) 4—Vicarious liability (115)

5—principal (116) 6—accessories before the fact(116) 7—principals in the second degree(116)

8—accomplices (116) 9—conspiracy (116) 10—Pinkerton (116) 11—*prima facie* (136)

12—strict liability (129) 13—mere presence (117) 14—accomplice liability (117)

15—accessory (116)

Chapter 6 Inchoate Crimes: Attempt, Conspiracy and Solicitation

LEARNING OBJECTIVES

After studying this chapter, students will

1. understand the concept of an inchoate crime.
2. know the functions of such crimes.
3. be familiar with the *actus reus* of attempt.
4. understand the *mens rea* of attempt.
5. be familiar with the impossibility defenses to attempt.
6. understand the basic idea of conspiracy.
7. understand the *actus reus* of conspiracy.
8. know the *mens rea* of conspiracy.
9. be familiar with the various approaches to conspiracy.
10. know the *mens rea* element of solicitation.
11. know the *actus reus* of solicitation.

KEYWORDS AND CONCEPTS

Criminal attempt—crime of starting but not completing some contemplated crime; p. 146
Criminal conspiracy—crime of agreeing to commit some planned crime; p. 146
Criminal solicitation—asking or hiring someone to commit a crime; p. 146
Inchoate offenses—incomplete offenses; p. 146
Dangerous conduct rationale—punish only attempters who come close to finishing; p. 148
Dangerous person rationale—punish only those who have shown they are dangerous; p. 148
General attempt statute—attempt statute that applies to other crimes in general; p. 149
Specific attempt statute—statutes covering an attempt to commit a specific crime; p. 149
Attempt *mens rea*—intent to complete a crime; p. 149
Attempt *actus reus*—acts necessary to create guilt for attempt; p. 155
Preparation—acts preliminary to an attempt; p. 155
Physical proximity test—focuses on how close attempter is to completing crime; p. 156
Unequivocality test—guilty of attempt only when acts confirm willingness to complete crime; p. 156
Model penal code test "substantial steps" test—defendant must have taken substantial steps before being guilty of attempt; p. 156
Indispensable element test—attempter has gotten control of everything needed to complete the crime; p. 156
Dangerous proximity test—has attempter come dangerously close to competing the crime; p. 156
Res ipsa loquitur test—attempters acts clearly indicate plan to commit a crime; p. 156
Legal impossibility defense—if attempter did all he wanted, it would not be a crime; p. 162
Factual impossibility defense—if attempter did all he wanted, completed crime still impossible; p. 162
Extraneous factor—factor that cause defendant from completing attempt; p. 162
Principle of legality—can punish only for acts officially defined as crimes; p. 162
Defense of voluntary abandonment—defendant voluntarily stopped the attempt; p. 170
Conspiracy—agreement to commit a crime; p. 174

Conspiracy *actus reus*—agreement, plus, in some states, an overt act pursuant to conspiracy; p. 174
Overt act—additional *actus reus* requirement for conspiracy in some jurisdictions; p. 175
Conspiracy *mens rea*—specific intent to commit a crime; p. 178
Unilateral approach—only one conspirator has to really agree or know of others; p. 179
Wheel conspiracies—one or more hub defendant participate in all agreements; p. 179
Chain conspiracies—participants deal only with others next to them in a chain; p. 179
RICO Act —federal Racketeer and Corrupt Organizations legislation; p.180
Solicitation—crime of inducing someone else to commit a crime; p. 181
Solicitation *actus reus*—making some effort to get another to commit a crime; p. 181
Solicitation *mens rea*—specific intent to commit a crime; p. 182

CHAPTER OUTLINE

I. Inchoate crimes are incomplete crimes.
  A. Inchoate comes from the Latin "to begin"
  B. Inchoate crimes are separate crimes of starting but not finishing any other crime.
  C. Whether to make it a crime to start but not finish committing a crime poses a problem:
    1. Is the law punishing someone who has done no harm or setting someone free who is determined to do harm?
    2. Dilemma of criminal attempt law is resolved through three requirements:
      a. Requiring specific intent.
      b. Requiring some action.
      c. Punishing inchoate crimes less severely than completed crimes.
  D. 3 types of inchoate offenses:
    1. Attempt—trying to commit a crime.
    2. Conspiracy—agreeing to commit a crime.
    3. Solicitation—trying to get someone else to commit a crime.
  E. All inchoate offenses are specific intent crimes.

II. An attempt is a failed effort to complete a crime.
  A. Attempt is the crime of trying but failing to commit a crime.
  B. Rationales for criminal attempt law:
    1. Prevent harm from dangerous conduct (focuses on how close to completion the crime is).
    2. Neutralize dangerous people (focuses on how developed the criminal purpose is).
    3. Both (1) and (2) look at actions taken to measure the danger.
  C. *Mens rea* of attempt
    1. Purpose or specific intent always present.
    2. No knowing, reckless, or negligent attempts
  D. *Actus reus* of attempt
    1. How much action is enough?
      a. Preparation isn't enough to qualify as the *actus reus* of attempt.

b. Toughest problem in criminal attempt: drawing line between preparation and attempt.

2. Tests to help draw the line between preparation and the act of attempt
    a. Physical proximity test
        (1) Focus on
            (a) Dangerous conduct, not dangerous people.
            (b) What's left to do, not what's already done.
        (2) Completion of all but the last act needed to accomplish the crime is surely enough, but so are acts falling short of this point, including:
            (a) Indispensable element test—defendants who've gotten control of everything they need to complete the crime.
            (b) Dangerous proximity test—defendants have gotten dangerously close to completing the crime.
    b. Unequivocality (probable desistance) test
        (1) Focus on
            (a) Dangerous persons, not dangerous conduct
            (b) What's already done, not what's left to do
        (2) Unequivocality test asks whether an ordinary person observing defendants' actions without knowing their intent would guess they were determined to commit the crime.
    c. "Substantial steps" (Model Penal Code) test
        (1) Purpose—clarify and simplify other tests
        (2) Focus on
            (a) Dangerous persons
            (b) What's already done, not what's left to do
        (3) Definition—substantial steps that "strongly corroborate" defendant's criminal purpose.

E. Impossibility of completing the crime as a defense
    1. Legal impossibility is a defense to criminal attempt; factual impossibility is not.
    2. Legal impossibility
        a. Defendants intend to commit crimes, do everything they can to complete the crime, but what they intend and do isn't a crime.
        b. Is a defense
    3. Factual impossibility
        a. Defendants' intend to commit a crime and take all the steps necessary to complete it, but a fact makes it impossible to complete.
        b. People bent on committing crimes shouldn't benefit from a stroke of luck—this isn't a defense.

F. Abandonment of attempts as a defense
    1. Complete and voluntary abandonment of attempts is an affirmative defense in about half the states.
    2. Arguments in favor of the abandonment defense
        a. People who voluntarily and completely give up their criminal attempts aren't dangerous.

b. We want to encourage people who are just about to hurt someone or their property to give up their plans.

3. Argument against defense of abandonment—it encourages bad people to take the early steps in committing crimes because they know they won't be punished.

III. Conspiracy is an agreement to commit a crime.
- A. Agreeing to commit crimes (criminal conspiracy) is further removed from completed crimes than trying to commit them (criminal attempt).
- B. Justifications for conspiracy law
  1. Works hand in hand with attempt to nip criminal purpose in the bud
  2. Strikes at the special danger of group criminal activity
- C. Conspiracy *actus reus*
  1. Agreement to commit a crime is the heart of the crime of conspiracy.
     - a. Doesn't have to be in writing
     - b. An unspoken understanding inferred from facts and circumstances is good enough to prove agreement.
  2. About half the states require an "overt act" in addition to the act of agreement.
     - a. Purpose—verify the firmness of the agreement
     - b. Act doesn't have to amount to much; it can be of "very small significance."
- D. Conspiracy *mens rea*
  1. Crime of purpose (specific intent)
  2. Can mean intent to make the agreement or intent to achieve the criminal objective.
- E. Parties to conspiracy
  1. Traditional approach—two or more individuals agreeing to commit crimes.
  2. Unilateral approach—not all the conspirators had to agree to commit a crime as long as the defendant believes they did.
- F. Large-scale conspiracies
  1. Wheel conspiracies: 2 sets of conspirators:
     - a. Hub—conspirators who participate in all transactions
     - b. Spokes—conspirators who only participate in one transaction
  2. Chain conspiracies—participants at one end of the chain don't know anything of participants at the other end, but they all handle the same illegal commodity at different points (manufacture, distribution, sale).
- G. Criminal objective of conspiracy
  1. Traditionally included everything from treason to disturbing the peace.
  2. Some effort to limit the reach of conspiracy
     - a. Requires an overt act in addition to an act of agreement
     - b. Applies to criminal objectives only

IV. Solicitation is asking or encouraging someone else to commit a crime.
- A. Definition—the crime of trying to get someone else to commit a crime.
- B. Arguments against criminal solicitation law

1. The act of soliciting isn't dangerous enough to punish because an independent moral force (the person solicited) stands between the solicitation and its objective.
2. Solicitors aren't dangerous enough people, and they prove it by needing someone else to do their dirty work.

C. Arguments for criminal solicitation law
1. Solicitation is another form of the danger of group criminality.
2. Solicitors are smart masters at manipulating others to do their dirty work.

D. Solicitation *actus reus* requires words that actually try to get someone to commit a crime (not just approve the commission of the crime).

E. Solicitation *mens rea* requires purpose or specific intent to get someone to commit a specific crime.

F. The objective of criminal solicitation varies from limiting it to violent felonies in some jurisdictions to including all crimes in other jurisdictions.

CHAPTER SUMMARY

Inchoate offenses involve punishing people for crimes they haven't completed. The term "inchoate" comes from the Latin "to begin." Inchoate offenses require some action but not enough to finish the crime intended. Such offenses enable the police, courts and corrections to intervene before the intended harm occurs. All of these offenses have both a general intent and a specific intent element. General intent is to do the act, say the words, make an agreement, etc. Specific intent is any intent other than general intent. In these crimes, the specific intent is to commit a crime above and beyond the inchoate offense. Inchoate crimes are generally punished separately and less severely than the completed offense.

Criminal liability for criminal attempt offenses is based on two rationales: First is preventing dangerous conduct, and second is neutralizing dangerous people. The *mens rea* of inchoate crimes is the specific intent to commit a complete crime.

The *actus reus* of attempt is an action that is beyond mere preparation but not completing the crime. How much action is required to make one guilty of an attempt is hotly debated and there are a number of approaches. A proximity approach focuses on how close the defendant gets to completing the crime. An unequivocality approach focuses on whether the defendant got far enough along that stopping is unlikely. The Model Penal Code test requires that the defendant have taken substantial steps and that such steps strongly corroborate the actor's criminal intent.

Legal impossibility is a defense to attempt liability. If the defendant did everything he or she wanted to do and it still wouldn't be a crime, then it is a valid defense. The principle of legality would seem to require this. Factual impossibility is not a defense. If certain factors unknown to the defendant would make it impossible to complete the crime, this is not a defense. In some jurisdictions voluntary and complete abandonment of an attempt in progress may be a defense to attempt liability.

Solicitation and conspiracy both involve more than one person. Punishing conspiracy and solicitation to commit a crime is based not only on preventing crime, but also on the special danger of group criminality.

Criminal conspiracy is the crime of agreeing with one or more people to commit a crime. The *actus reus* of conspiracy is the agreement. Some jurisdictions also require that one of the coconspirators commit some overt act in pursuance of the conspiracy. Conspiracy is a specific intent crime. In addition to intending to agree (general intent), they must also intend to commit the planned crime.

The traditional approach to conspiracy required that at least two people really and sincerely agree to commit a crime (bilateral approach). Under this approach, a person could not be guilty of conspiring with an undercover police officer that had no intent to agree or carry out a crime. Under the unilateral approach, there can be a conspiracy even though another party does not truly agree and doesn't even know some of the others involved.

Criminal solicitation is the crime of trying to get one or more persons to commit a crime. The *actus reus* is a solicitation, command, or encouragement to commit a crime. In addition to a general intent to ask or command, there must be a specific intent that the solicited crime be completed.

PRACTICE TEST BANK

Multiple Choice

1. The term inchoate comes from the Latin verb which means "to _____."
   a. contemplate
   b. envision
   c. begin
   d. conspire

2. All inchoate crimes are _____ crimes.
   a. specific and general intent
   b. circumstances
   c. capital
   d. redemptive

3. As compared to the completed crime, inchoate crimes are _____.
   a. always misdemeanors
   b. punished the same as the completed crime
   c. more severely punished than the completed crime
   d. less severely punished than the completed crime

4. The rationales for attempt focus on two different types of danger, _____.
   a. group activity and inciting others
   b. dangerous persons and dangerous conduct
   c. imitation and stimulation of crime
   d. group activity and stimulation of crime

5. The indispensable element test of attempt *actus reus* focuses on whether the actor _____.
   a. is likely to give up the attempt
   b. had gotten control of everything necessary to complete the crime
   c. satisfies the *res ipsa loquitur* criterion
   d. is just one step away from completing the crime

6. The Latin term *res ipsa loquitur* means the _____.
   a. thing is inherently evil
   b. thought is the origin of the act
   c. act speaks for itself
   d. intent without action is no crime

7. The Model Penal Code test of attempt *actus reus* requires that the defendant take ______ toward completing the crime.
   a. irreversible action
   b. substantial steps
   c. the last proximate act
   d. the next-to-last proximate act

8. The second part of the Model Penal Code test of attempt *actus reus* also requires that the defendant's actions _____.
   a. go beyond any reasonable stopping point
   b. indicate that desistance is unlikely
   c. indicate that they are dangerously close to completing the offense
   d. strongly corroborate intent to commit the crime

9. In most states, and under the Model Penal Code, which of the following would not be an attempt?
   a. lying in wait for the victim to walk by
   b. reconnoitering the planned crime scene
   c. enticing the victim to the place where the crime is planned to occur
   d. beginning to gather the materials necessary for the crime

10. The defense of ____ impossibility involves actors doing everything they can to carry out the criminal intent, but the law doesn't criminalize what they did.
   a. factual
   b. virtual
   c. legal
   d. juristic

11. The defense of _____ impossibility involves the situation where some extraneous factor interrupts or prevents completion of the crime.
    a. factual
    b. virtual
    c. real
    d. legal

12. Which of the following is a recognized form of the impossibility defense to attempt?
    a. legal
    b. factual
    c. real
    d. virtual

13. According to the appellate court in State v. Damms, a defendant can be guilty of the crime of attempted murder because/even though the defendant admitted to police that he _____.
    a. believed the gun was loaded (even though it was in fact unloaded)
    b. believed his wife was already dead (even though she wasn't)
    c. believed the wounds would not be fatal (even though they were)
    d. believed the police would stop him before he pointed the gun at this wife

14. Which of the following would be a valid impossibility defense?
    a. The intended victim escapes before the defendant attacks the victim.
    b. The defendant is apprehended by the police before finishing the crime.
    c. The poison is not strong enough to kill the victim.
    d. What the defendant wants to do to the victim is not a crime.

15. To be a defense to attempt, the abandonment of the attempt must be _____.
    a. caused by an extraneous factor
    b. compelled
    c. voluntary
    d. caused by police intervention

16. About half the states have a second *actus reus* element for conspiracy. They require that _____.
    a. the conspirators take a substantial step toward the crime
    b. the conspirators move beyond mere preparation
    c. one of the conspirators attempt the crime
    d. one of the conspirators do an overt act pursuant to the conspiracy

17. Mr. X conspires with Mr. Y to commit a murder. Unbeknownst to Mr. X, Y is an undercover police officer that is only trying to build a case against X. Under the unilateral approach to conspiracy, _____.
   a. both X and Y are guilty of conspiracy
   b. X is not guilty of conspiracy because there is no real agreement
   c. X has an affirmative defense
   d. X is guilty of conspiracy

18. Chain conspiracies usually involve _____.
   a. a distributor who sells to numerous dealers
   b. a smuggler who has a number of wholesale customers
   c. a dealer who has multiple customers
   d. a pipeline from a smuggler to a distributor to a wholesaler

19. Most modern conspiracy statutes _____.
   a. limit the objective to committing a crime
   b. include any objective which is contrary to public policy
   c. limit the objective to using unlawful means to do a lawful thing
   d. include any objective which is injurious to public health

20. The federal _____ Act is a specialized conspiracy law frequently utilized against organized crime.
   a. PACO
   b. RICO
   c. CHACO
   d. OCCA

21. Which of the following is not a typical element of solicitation statutes?
   a. general intent
   b. specific intent
   c. communicating some inducement
   d. communication must be to a particular person

22. A few states restrict the crime of solicitation to solicitation of _____.
   a. felonies
   b. misdemeanors
   c. capital felonies
   d. crimes which are *mala prohibita*

23. Which of the following is required to obtain a solicitation conviction?
   a. the person solicited must accept the offer
   b. the solicitor must have specific intent
   c. the solicitor and solicitee must enter into a conspiracy
   d. the person solicited must commit the crime

24. At common law, the crime of attempt _____.
   a. did not exist
   b. had no specific intent element
   c. required some injury
   d. required that the defendant do the last proximate act

25. Physical proximity tests of attempt *actus reus* focus on _____.
   a. how close the defendant got to completing the crime
   b. whether a reasonable person would see that a crime is in progress
   c. whether the defendant is likely to cease the attempt
   d. how much of the defendant's intent is shown by action

26. The unequivocality test of attempt *actus reus* focuses on _____.
   a. whether the defendant is likely to give up the attempt
   b. how much remains to be done before completing the crime
   c. whether the defendant has taken substantial steps
   d. whether the defendant has started preparing for the crime

27. The Model Penal Code test of attempt *actus reus* focuses on _____.
   a. probable desistance and unequivocality
   b. steps taken by the defendant and unequivocality
   c. intent and steps taken by the defendant.
   d. *res ipsa loquitur* and intent

28. According to the Model Penal Code, soliciting an innocent agent to commit the crime is _____.
   a. an attempted conspiracy
   b. an attempted solicitation
   c. an attempt
   d. a conspiracy

29, Unlike the early common law approach to attempt, the law today does not require _____.
   a. that any or partial harm be caused on inflicted
   b. any specific intent
   c. any general intent
   d. that there be any *actus reus*

30. At common law, an attempted capital offense such as robbery, murder or burglary _____.
   a. was executed
   b. was sentenced to life in prison
   c. was guilty of a non-capital felony
   d. was guilty only of a misdemeanor

True-False

1. All inchoate offenses have a specific intent element.
   a. true
   b. false

2. Inchoate crimes are punished at the same level as the object or completed crime.
   a. true
   b. false

3. Attempt was not a crime at common law.
   a. true
   b. false

4. There are no such things as reckless, negligent or strict liability attempts.
   a. true
   b. false

5. An attempt requires more than mere preparation to commit the crime.
   a. true
   b. false

6. The Model Penal Code definition of the *actus reus* of attempt is an example of the probable desistance approach.
   a. true
   b. false

7. Legal impossibility is a defense to the crime of attempt.
   a. true
   b. false

8. Factual impossibility is a valid defense to the crime of attempt.
   a. true
   b. false

9. The Model Penal Code *actus reus* of attempt involves substantial steps that strongly corroborate the actor's criminal purpose.
   a. true
   b. false

10. A person cannot be convicted of attempting to murder someone with a pistol if the pistol was, in fact, unloaded at the time.
    a. true
    b. false

11. To be a valid defense, the abandonment of an attempt must be voluntary.
   a. true
   b. false

12. In some jurisdictions, there are two act elements in the crime of conspiracy.
   a. true
   b. false

13. The offense of conspiracy is frequently criticized because of its vagueness.
   a. true
   b. false

14. The fact that one conspirator has been acquitted does not prevent the government from prosecuting the others for conspiracy.
   a. true
   b. false

15. In most modern conspiracy statutes, the criminal objective is usually limited to agreements to commit crimes.
   a. true
   b. false

16. RICO stands for Racketeer Influenced and Corrupt Organizations.
   a. true
   b. false

17. In some jurisdictions, the crime of solicitation is limited to solicitation to commit misdemeanors.
   a. true
   b. false

18. A solicitation that does not reach or is not heard by the intended recipient cannot be a crime.
   a. true
   b. false

19. To be criminal, a solicitation must be directed toward a specific individual.
   a. true
   b. false

20. The crime of solicitation is a strict liability crime.
   a. true
   b. false

21. In a wheel conspiracy, one or more defendants participate in every transaction.
    a. true
    b. false

22. A person can be guilty of conspiracy even though they do not know all of the others in the conspiracy.
    a. true
    b. false

23. The Model Penal Code definition of conspiracy includes an overt act element.
    a. true
    b. false

24. For the solicitor to be guilty of solicitation, the person solicited must accept the offer.
    a. true
    b. false

25. The primary purpose of requiring some overt act in some conspiracy statutes is to help identify who is involved in the conspiracy.
    a. true
    b. false

<u>Fill in the blank</u>

1. Under the ________________ test, an attempt has been committed when the person has gotten control of everything they need to complete the crime.

2. Abandonment is not a defense to attempt unless the abandonment is ____________.

3. In some states, the second *actus reus* requirement is that there be an ____________ act by one of the conspirators in pursuance of the conspiracy.

4. The term __________________________ means "the thing stands for itself."

5. _____________ impossibility is not a valid defense to attempt.

6. The _________________ test of attempt *actus reus* focuses on how close the defendant got to completing the crime.

7. Acts toward committing a crime that do not constitute an attempt are called ________ _______________.

8. In the _______________ approach to conspiracy, a person can be guilty even though no one else in the conspiracy really agrees to commit the crime.

9. Under the ____________ approach to attempt *actus reus*, the test is whether the acts confirm the intent.

10. ____________ impossibility is a defense to attempt.

11. RICO means ____.

12. In a ____________ conspiracy, one or more defendants participate in all transactions.

13. Of the inchoate offenses, only ____________ is sometimes defined as having two act elements.

14. ____________ can be thought of as the first half of a conspiracy.

15. The principle of ____________ leads to the conclusion that legal impossibility is a defense to attempt.

<u>Essay</u>

1. Define, describe, compare and contrast conspiracy, attempt and solicitation. Be sure to provide an example of each.

2. Discuss the various approaches to the *actus reus* of attempt. Provide an example of each.

3. Define, describe, compare and contrast legal and factual impossibility as defenses to attempt.

4. How does the legal impossibility defense relate to the principle of legality?

5. How has the law of attempt changed since early common law?

CHAPTER 6 ANSWER KEY

Multiple Choice

1—c (146)	2—a (146)	3—d (141)	4—b (148)	5—b (156)
6—c (156)	7—b (157)	8—d (157)	9—d (157)	10—c (162)
11—b (162)	12—c (162)	13—a (165)	14—d (162)	15—c (170)
16—d (174)	17—d (179)	18—d (179)	19—a (180)	20—b (180)
21—d (182)	22—a (182)	23—a (182)	24—c (147)	25—a (156)
26—a (156)	27—c (156)	28—c (157)	29—a (147-9)	30—a (147)

True-False

1—T (146)	2—F (146)	3—F (147)	4—T (149)	5—T (155)
6—F (157)	7—T (162)	8—F (162)	9—T (157)	10—F (164)
11—T (170)	12—T (174)	13—T (178)	14—T (179)	15—T (180)
16—T (180)	17—F (182)	18—F (182)	19—F (182)	20—F (182)
21—T (179)	22—T (179)	23—T (180)	24—F (182)	25—F (175)

Fill in the blank

1—indispensable element (156) 2—voluntary (170) 3—overt (175) 4—*res ipsa loquitur* (156)

5—factual (162) 6—physical proximity (156) 7—mere preparation (155)

8—unilateral (179) 9—unequivocality (156) 10—legal (162)

11—Racketeer Influenced and Corrupt Organizations (180)

12—wheel (179) 13—conspiracy (175) 14—solicitation (181) 15—legality (162)

Chapter 7 Defenses to Liability: Justifications

LEARNING OBJECTIVES

After studying this chapter, students will

1. know the three basic kinds of defenses.
2. understand the concept of justification.
3. be familiar with the burden of proof and burden of persuasion.
4. understand the basic rules of use of force and deadly force.
5. know when retreat is or is not required before using deadly force.
6. be familiar with the lawful use of force to defend others.
7. understand the rules on use of force to defend home and property.
8. be familiar with the choice-of-evils defense.
9. understand the defense of consent.

KEY TERMS AND CONCEPTS

Alibi—defense that defendant was elsewhere at time crime committed; p. 191
Principle of justification—defense that acts were justified or right under the circumstances; p. 191
Principle of excuse—defense that they shouldn't be held responsible; p. 192
Affirmative defenses—defendant must put in some evidence of defense; p. 192
Burden of production—obligation to put in some evidence of a defense or other matter; p. 192
Burden of persuasion—obligation to prove (or disprove) a defense or other matter; p. 192
Preponderance of the evidence—typical burden of persuasion for affirmative defenses; p. 192
Perfect defenses—defense that requires acquittal; p. 192
Imperfect defenses—defense that reduces conviction to a lesser offense; p. 192
Mitigating circumstances—circumstances that may reduce punishment; p. 192
Motive—reason for committing crime; may be element or mitigating circumstance; p. 193
Unprovoked attack—self-defense generally not available if defendant made attack; p. 194
Imminent danger—use of force justified to defend only if harm will be immediate; p. 194
Necessity—need to defend against attack right now; p. 194
Reasonable force—amount objectively reasonable under the circumstances to defend; p. 194
Initial aggressor—person who started fight; usually cannot use self-defense; p. 194
Withdrawal exception—initial aggressor can use self-defense if they stop the attack completely; p. 194
Serious (grievous) bodily injury—threat that justifies defensive use of deadly force; p. 196
Present danger—force may be used only to defend against an imminent threat; p. 205
Retreat rule—general rule that one must retreat if it can be done safely before using deadly force; p. 214
Stand-your-ground rule—rule in some jurisdictions that retreat is not required; p. 214
Castle exception—defender not required to retreat from or in own home; p. 214
Curtilage—area immediately outside home including lawn; p. 219
Choice-of-evils defense—necessity defense; committing crime resulted in net social good; p. 223
General principle of necessity—same as choice-of-evils defense; p. 223
Voluntary consent—defense available to some offenses; defendant agreed to the offense; p. 230

Knowing consent—consent is valid only if person knew what was involved in the consent; p. 230

Authorized consent—person giving consent was authorized to do so; p. 230

CHAPTER OUTLINE

I. There are a variety of defenses to criminal liability.
- A. There are three legitimate types:
  1. Alibi—defendant proves it was impossible for him to have committed the crime because defendant was elsewhere.
  2. Justification—defendant responsible, but the act was justified.
  3. Excuse—defendant did it, but isn't responsible for his action.
- B. Affirmative defenses are a type of defense.
  1. In some jurisdictions, defendants have some responsibility to prove their affirmative defenses.
  2. In other jurisdictions, government has some responsibility to disprove such defenses.
- C. Results of defendants' successful proof of defense
  1. Perfect defenses—an acquittal results.
  2. Imperfect defenses—reduce the crime to a lesser offense.
  3. Mitigating circumstances—reduce the penalty for the crime.
- D. Motive can be an element and/or influence punishment.

II. Justification defenses are based on necessity.
- A. Necessity and the rule of law
  1. Government has the monopoly on force under the rule of law.
  2. Necessity justifies violating the rule of law by allowing individuals to take the law into their own hands.
  3. Strictly limited to situations that meet three conditions:
     - a. The necessity is great.
     - b. The danger of harm is imminent.
     - c. For prevention only.
- B. There are five types of justification defenses.
  1. Self-defense
  2. Defense of others
  3. Defense of home and property
  4. Choice-of-evils defense
  5. Defense of consent

III. Self-defense is a justification for the use of force.
- A. The elements of self-defense
  1. Unprovoked attack (total withdrawal by attacker an exception)
  2. Honest and reasonable belief in imminent danger of death or serious bodily injury
  3. Honest and reasonable belief in the need to defend against attack right now—imminent or present danger

        4. Reasonable (not excessive) force to repel attack
    B. The retreat doctrine may limit self-defense.
        1. Two rules
            a. You have to retreat if escape is reasonable (most states).
            b. If you didn't start the fight, you can stand your ground even if you could escape by retreating (a few states).
        2. Castle exception—retreat from/in home not required; you can stand your ground.

IV. The defense of others is a justification for the use of force.
    A. Who is included
        1. Most states include individuals in a "special relationship."
        2. Some states include anyone in imminent danger of harm.
    B. Defense applies only to those who can claim the right to defend themselves.

V. The defense of home and property is a justification for the use of force.
    A. Rooted in ancient idea that our home is our castle.
    B. Extension of the right of self-defense
    C. Limits to using deadly force vary by state.
        1. Must have reasonable belief intruders intend to commit:
            a. Violent felonies against occupants
            b. Any felony
            c. Any offense
        2. Area covered
            a. Entry into occupied home
            b. Entry into curtilage

VI. The choice-of-evils defense is a justification defense.
    A. Basic idea—immediate necessity justifies choosing to commit a lesser crime to avoid the harm of a greater crime.
    B. Elements
        1. Identify evils (usually in legislation)
        2. Rank evils (usually in legislation)
        3. Choose the lesser evil to avoid imminent harm from the greater evil.

VII. The defense of consent is a justification for some crimes.
    A. Justification—the value of individual autonomy in a free society
    B. Consent is not a defense, but there are four exceptions:
        1. No serious injury results from consent.
        2. Injury occurs during sporting events.
        3. Consent benefits the person who consents (patient consents to surgery).
        4. Consent is a defense to certain sex crimes.
    C. Exceptions are necessary to the defense but are not enough unless consent is also voluntary and knowing.

CHAPTER SUMMARY

There are three kinds of defenses: alibis, justifications, and excuses. Alibis free defendants from criminal liability, because they prove it's impossible for the defendants to have committed the crime because they were somewhere else at the time of the crime. Justifications free defendants from criminal liability, because they prove the defendants aren't blameworthy. Doing the criminal acts was right or justified. An example is self-defense. Excuses free defendants from criminal liability, because they prove the defendants aren't responsible for their acts. An example is the insanity defense.

All the justification defenses are exceptions to the rule of law. They allow individuals to take the law into their own hands. According to the rule of law, the government has a monopoly on the use of force. Use of force by individuals must be justified by law.

Self-defense is a concession to necessity and is only justified when the force is reasonably and immediately necessary for defense. Deadly force is justified only when the necessity is unprovoked and the attack involves threatened death or serious bodily injury. The amount of force used must be the minimum amount reasonably necessary to defend against an imminent threat. The general rule is that a person must retreat if they can safely do so before using deadly force. This rule puts a premium on human life—even the life of an attacker. The castle exception and the rules regarding the defense of home clearly demonstrate the ancient doctrine that homes are castles is still alive and well. In general, a person is not required to retreat from or in their own home before using deadly force.

The right to defend others includes everyone from close family members to any stranger who needs immediate protection from attack. The same rules apply as in self-defense.

The choice-of-evils defense is also based on necessity. This defense protects those who make the right choice in deciding to commit a lesser crime to avoid the imminent harm of a greater crime or social harm. The crime results in a net social good.

The general rule is that consent by the victim is not a defense. However, consent is a defense to some crimes in some circumstances. The consent must be knowing and voluntary. The value of individual autonomy (not necessity) is the heart of the defense of consent.

PRACTICE TEST BANK

Multiple Choice

1. Which of the following is not one of the three types of legal defenses to crime?
    a. alibi
    b. justifications
    c. excuses
    d. mitigating circumstances

2. The current approach to self defense requires that the defender _____.
    a. ward off future attacks by using a pre-emptive strike
    b. reasonably believe in the danger of an imminent attack
    c. use whatever amount of force the defender subjectively thinks is justified
    d. have provoked the incident

3. In justification defenses, defendants admit they did the act but seek acquittal on the ground that their acts _____.
    a. were right
    b. were wrong, but they shouldn't be held responsible
    c. were not done purposely
    d. were done accidentally

4. The amount of force that the law allows to be used in self-defense is the minimum amount _____.
    a. reasonably excessive
    b. reasonably necessary
    c. unreasonably sufficient
    d. inversely proportionate

5. Under the castle exception to the retreat doctrine, the defender does not have to retreat before using defensive force if they _____.
    a. were the initial aggressor
    b. were verbally provoked by the attacker
    c. are attacked in their own home
    d. have already retreated once

6. The "choice-of-evils" defense is also known as the _____.
    a. public duty defense
    b. rational behavior defense
    c principle or defense of necessity
    d. rational person test

7. In general, consent is _____.
   a. not a defense to crime
   b. a defense only to crimes resulting in death or serious bodily injury
   c. not a defense to intentional or purposeful crime
   d. a defense only if the conduct that causes injury has no benefit to society

8. The most famous English case involving choice of evils defense was _____.
   a. The Queen v. Dunn and Bradstreet.
   b. The Queen v. Bradley and Clemens.
   c. The Queen v. Cooper and Lybrands.
   d. The Queen v. Dudley and Stephens.

9. The reason why a person commits a crime is called _____.
   a. the motive
   b. the *mens rea*
   c. an excuse
   d. a justification

10 A consent defense to a charge of assault is most likely to succeed when _____.
   a. the assaulter is weaker and smaller than the victim
   b. the assault occurs in a lawful sporting event
   c. the victim is already injured
   d. the consent is given after the assault

11. In order for the consent of the victim to be a valid defense, the consent must be _____.
   a. knowing and subjective
   b. voluntary and objective
   c. in writing
   d. voluntary and knowing

12. Which of the following is a step in the Model Penal Code approach to the choice of evils defense?
   a. compare the possible sentences for the two crimes involved
   b. rank the culpability involved in the two offenses at issue
   c. rank the harms
   d. choose the greater evil to avoid the lesser evil

13. To have a valid claim of using force to defend another person, the defendant must show that _____.
   a. the attacker also threatened to use force against the defender
   b. the person defended had a right to use force to defend themselves
   c. the use of force by the attacker against the victim was lawful
   d. the defender must be stronger than the person attacked

14. In State v. Stewart, Mrs. Steward killed her husband while he was asleep. She argued self-defense. On appeal, the court concluded that Mrs. Stewart _____.
    a. did not act in self-defense because she failed to prove that she suffered from battered woman syndrome
    b. was not entitled to the defense because she had other options besides killing
    c. was not entitled to defend herself because she used deadly force
    d. did not act in self-defense because the threat to her from her husband was not imminent

15. One of the most controversial self-defense cases of the 1980's occurred in the New York subway. The defendant was _____.
    a. Troy Canty
    b. Barry Allen
    c. Darrell Caby
    d. Bernhard Goetz

16. The party that has the burden of persuasion on an issue must _____.
    a. prove the point or lose on the issue
    b. present some evidence to get the issue into the case
    c. inform the jury before trial that they will raise the issue
    d. present enough evidence to meet the burden of production

17. The appellate court in State v. Shelly and the Model Penal Code limit the use of the consent defense to sporting activities where the injury and conduct are _____.
    a. reasonably foreseeable hazards
    b. a felony offense
    c. specifically agreed to before the contest begins
    d. permitted by the rules of the game

18. Nearly all states allow the use of deadly force in some circumstances to _____.
    a. resist a lawful arrest
    b. protect their home
    c. stop a person committing any type of misdemeanor in the home
    d. stop a person from committing a felony in a public place

19. A defense in which defendants admit the act but claim they aren't legally responsible is called a/n _____.
    a. justification
    b. claim of right
    c. mitigating condition
    d. excuse

20. If the defendant establishes a perfect defense, the defendant _____.
    a. is committed to a mental hospital
    b. may still be convicted of a lesser offense
    c. is entitled to be found not guilty
    d. is entitled to a reduced sentence

21. A defendant is charged with murder, but manages to get a conviction on manslaughter. This can occur if a defendant establishes certain types of _____.
    a. justifications
    b. excuses
    c. mitigating circumstances
    d. imperfect defenses

22. In most, if not all countries, including the U.S., the government claims a _____ on the legitimate use of force and authorizes private use of force only in certain circumstances.
    a. franchise
    b. lien
    c. trust
    d. monopoly

23. In most jurisdictions, the defendant's belief that self-defense was necessary must be sincere and _____.
    a. objectively reasonable
    b. subjectively unreasonable
    c. empirically accurate
    d. empirically verifiable

24. Defensive force may be used lawfully only if the danger is _____.
    a. foreseeable
    b. imminent
    c. mandatory
    d. contingent

25. The general rule is that self-defense is lawfully available only against ____ attacks.
    a. unprovoked
    b. justified
    c. legal
    d. excusable

26. Persons who are the initial, unprovoked aggressor can acquire a lawful right to defend themselves if they __________ from the fight they started.
    a. foreseeably desist
    b. irrevocably renounce themselves
    c. contingently abstain
    d. completely withdraw

27. The true man rule for retreat before using force is also known as the _____ rule.
    a. castle
    b. stand-your-ground
    c. reasonable retreat
    d. foreseeable desistance

28. Which of the following defenses, if established, typically does not result in an acquittal or conviction of a lesser offense?
    a. insanity
    b. self-defense
    c. necessity
    d. choice-of-evils

29. Circumstances about the crime that may reduce the punishment are called _____ circumstances.
    a. contingent
    b. foreseeable
    c. mitigating
    d. compensatory

30. Justifications focus on the _____.
    a. personal accountability of the defendant
    b. the rightfulness of an otherwise criminal act
    c. legal responsibility of the defendant
    d. mitigating circumstances

True/False

1. A perfect defense leads to an acquittal.
    a. true
    b. false

2. It is never lawful to use force to protect property.
    a. true
    b. false

3. Preemptive strikes at a potential attacker are valid self-defense.
    a. true
    b. false

4. Consent is never a defense to any sex crime.
    a. true
    b. false

5. The term "motive" means the same as "intent."
   a. true
   b. false

6. In the alibi defense, defendants argue that they were somewhere else at the time of the crime and not at the scene of the crime.
   a. true
   b. false

7. Retaliation for past attacks or threats justifies defensive use of force.
   a. true
   b. false

8. There is no defense to using force against someone who is not attacking the actor but is attacking some other person.
   a. true
   b. false

9. Defendants prove most defenses beyond a reasonable doubt.
   a. true
   b. false

10. If the convicted defendant shows mitigating circumstances, they may be able to get a reduced sentence.
   a. true
   b. false

11. Insanity is an example of an excuse defense.
   a. true
   b. false

12. In both excuses and justifications, the defendant admits doing the *actus reus*.
   a. true
   b. false

13. The burden of production is on the defendant for affirmative defenses.
   a. true
   b. false

14. Imperfect self-defense, may, in some jurisdictions reduce a murder to manslaughter.
   a. true
   b. false

15. The reason why the person commits the crime is called the motive.
   a. true
   b. false

16. In all states, a person must retreat from their home if they can safely do so before using deadly force.
    a. true
    b. false

17. A person cannot lawfully use force to prevent an anticipated attack.
    a. true
    b. false

18. No matter what may happen later, the initial attacker can never claim self-defense.
    a. true
    b. false

19. The Model Penal Code recognizes a choice-of-evils defense.
    a. true
    b. false

20. The choice-of-evils defense requires that the defendant have correctly identified and weighed the evils.
    a. true
    b. false

21. The choice-of-evils defense was available at common law.
    a. true
    b. false

22. The outside area immediately surrounding the home is called the curtilage.
    a. true
    b. false

23. At common law, the right to use deadly force to defend your own home was not recognized.
    a. true
    b. false

24. In many jurisdictions, deadly force can be used to defend yourself against certain serious felonies.
    a. true
    b. false

25. Consent is a defense to all crimes.
    a. true
    b. false

Fill in the blank

1. Only the danger of a/n ____________ attack justifies the use of force in self-defense.

2. Under the ____________ exception to the retreat doctrine, one does not have to retreat in one's own home before using defensive force.

3. To have a valid claim of self-defense, the actor must have had an honest and ____________ belief in the necessity of using force.

4. Abused wives who use force against their abusive husbands will frequently argue that the wife suffered from ______________________________________.

5. The law regarding defense of homes is influenced by the common-law idea that person's home is their ____________.

6. The criminal law generally excludes the defense of ____________, where serious injury is inflicted on the victim.

7. Running a stop sign to get a seriously ill person to the hospital would be an example of the ____________ defense.

8. A/n ____________ defense is one that reduces, but does not eliminate, criminal liability.

9. The duty to retreat before using deadly force is weakest when the person is attacked in their ____________.

10. The lawn and or other space immediately outside the home is called the ____________.

11. The ____________ is the reason for committing crime.

12. ____________ circumstances are circumstances which may lead to a reduction in sentence.

13. The true man rule is also known as the ______________________________ rule.

14. A/n ______________ defense is one that, if established, requires a verdict of not guilty.

15. The burden of proof or ____________ is a party's obligation to finally prove (or disprove) a defense or other matter.

Essay

1. Define, describe, compare and contrast justifications and excuses. Be sure to give an example of each.

2. Discuss the defense of consent. Be sure to provide examples.

3. Discuss fully the choice-of-evils defense and present an example of where the defense would be valid and one example where it would not be valid.

4. Discuss the general rules on the use of force and deadly force and retreat. Be sure to provide examples.

5. What is the battered woman('s) syndrome and how do abused women attempt to use their affliction with this in their defense for killing an abusive spouse?

CHAPTER 7 ANSWER KEY

Multiple Choice

1—d (192)	2—b (194)	3—a (192)	4—b (194)	5—c (214)
6—c (223)	7—a (230)	8—d (224)	9—a (193)	10—b (230)
11—d (230)	12—b (224)	13—b (217)	14—d (208)	15—d (201)
16—d (192)	17—a (232)	18—b (218)	19—d (192)	20—c (192)
21—d (192)	22—d (193)	23—a (194)	24—b (205)	25—a (194)
26—b (194)	27—b (214)	28—a (192)	29—c (192)	30—b (192)

True-False

1—T (192)	2—F (223)	3—F (194)	4—F (230)	5—F (193)
6—T (191)	7—F (194)	8—F (217)	9—F (192)	10—T (192)
11—T (192)	12—T (192)	13—T (192)	14—T (192)	15—T (193)
16—F (214)	17—T (194)	18—F (194)	19—T (224)	20—T (224)
21—T (203)	22—T (219)	23—F (218)	24—T (196)	25—F (230)

Fill in the blank

1—imminent (194) 2—castle (214) 3—reasonable (194) 4—battered woman syndrome (208)

5—castle (214) 6—consent (230) 7—choice-of evils (223) 8—imperfect (192)

9—home (214) 10—curtilage (219) 11—motive (193) 12— mitigating (192)

13—stand-your-ground (214) 14—perfect (192) 15—persuasion

Chapter 8 Defenses to Criminal Liability: Excuses

LEARNING OBJECTIVES

After studying this chapter, students will

1. understand the basic idea of excuses.
2. understand the insanity defense.
3. know the basic types of insanity defense.
4. be familiar with the defense of diminished capacity.
5. understand the common law and current approach to age as a defense.
6. be familiar with the duress defense.
7. understand voluntary and involuntary intoxication as defenses.
8. be familiar with the two main versions of the entrapment defense.
9. understand the concept of syndromes and when these can be defenses.

KEY TERMS AND CONCEPTS

Insanity—defense to crime based on mental illness; p. 240
Civil commitment—frequently results after verdict of not guilty by reason of insanity; p. 240
Cognition—focus of some insanity tests; what the defendant knows or appreciates; p. 241
Volition—focus of some insanity test; examines defendant's self-control or will; p. 241
Right-wrong test (M'Naghten rule)—traditional insanity test focusing on cognition; p. 241
Mental disease—insanity must be caused by a recognized mental disease; p. 241
Mental defect—insanity must be caused by a recognized mental defect; p. 242
Nature and quality of the act—part of M'Naghten test focuses on knowing these; 242
Product test—short-lived insanity test used only two jurisdictions; p. 244
Durham rule—another name for product test; was crime product of mental illness; p. 244
Irresistible impulse test—insanity test focusing on volition; p. 245
Substantial capacity test—Model Penal Code test of insanity; p. 246
Burden of proof—designated which party must prove or disprove a defense; p. 252
Diminished capacity—partial defense that negates *mens rea*; p. 252
Irrebuttable presumption—presumption that cannot be challenged or rebutted; p. 253
Duress (defense of)—defendant committed crime under serious threat from another; p. 258
Intoxication—is a defense if involuntary, not a defense if voluntary; p. 262
Entrapment (defense of)—defense based on improper police inducement; p.267
Syndrome—collection of symptoms associated with a particular disease or condition; p.272

CHAPTER OUTLINE

I. Excuses are a form of defense to a criminal charge.
- A. Difference between justification and excuse
    - 1. Justification— admits responsibility, but, under the circumstances, claims it was the right thing.
    - 2. Excuse—admits doing wrong but, under the circumstances, claims not legally responsible.

B. Circumstances affecting responsibility
   1. *Actus reus*—the act was involuntary.
   2. *Mens rea*—a mental disease or defect left defendant unable to form criminal intent.

C. Origins of circumstances
   1. Some people have a mental disease or defect or their age impairs their mental abilities.
      a. Insanity
      b. Diminished capacity
      c. Age
   2. Abnormal situations may result in an excuse for criminal conduct.
      a. Duress
      b. Intoxication
      c. Entrapment
      d. Various syndromes

II. Insanity is a defense based on a defendant's mental disease or defect.

A. Definition—defendant was so mentally diseased, he couldn't know nature of acts or control actions.

B. A legal, but not a medical, concept

C. Rationale—can't blame people who aren't responsible.

D. Consequence— civil commitment, not freedom

E. Tests
   1. Right-wrong test elements
      a. Mental disease (psychosis) or defect (retardation) damaged reason at the time of the crime.
      b. Defendant didn't know (simple awareness).
         (1) Nature of actions
         (2) Right or wrong
            (a) Legal wrong
            (b) Moral wrong
   2. Product-of-mental illness test elements (Durham rule)
      a. Checks for both reason and will
      b. Acts that are a product of mental illness excuse criminal liability.
   3. Irresistible impulse test elements
      a. Defendant had a mental disease or defect at the time of the crime.
      b. Defendant knew the nature of act and knew it was wrong.
      c. The mental disease or defect caused an impulse he couldn't control (volitional failure).
   4. Substantial capacity test elements (Model Penal Code)
      a. The mental disease or defect damages either or both reason and will.
      b. The mental disease or defect causes
         (1) Substantial (not complete) lack of reason and control
         (2) Failure to appreciate (not just purely intellectual awareness of) nature or wrongfulness
         (3) Failure to conform behavior to law

F. Burden of proof
   1. Former federal standard (Hinckley case)
      a. Government has to prove sanity beyond a reasonable doubt.
      b. Defense has only to raise a reasonable doubt about sanity.
   2. Most states—affirmative defense
      a. Defendant must show some evidence of insanity.
      b. Government then has to prove sanity (in varying levels, depending on the jurisdiction).
         (1) Beyond a reasonable doubt
         (2) With clear and convincing evidence
         (3) By a preponderance of the evidence

III. The diminished capacity defense negates intent.
   A. Mental disease or defect diminishes capacity but not enough to qualify as insanity defense.
   B. Limited to diseases or defects that make it impossible to form the intent required to commit the crime.

IV. Age is a defense or a basis for juvenile court jurisdiction.
   A. Immaturity excuses criminal liability.
   B. Age of maturity varies, but three stages at common law and later:
      1. Early childhood—can't form criminal intent (irrebuttable presumption).
      2. Middle childhood—rebuttable presumption against capacity to form intent.
      3. Adult—conclusive presumption of capacity to form intent.
   C. Age can aggravate as well as excuse criminal responsibility.
   D. Young offenders in all jurisdictions may be subject to the jurisdiction of juvenile courts for certain offenses.

V. Duress is a defense involving a person being threatened if they don't commit a crime.
   A. Definition—defendants who commit crimes because they're threatened with harm if they don't.
   B. Three grounds for the defense:
      1. No voluntary *actus reus*
      2. No *mens rea*
      3. Sound public policy
   C. Elements
      1. Qualifying crimes vary from minor to serious (never for homicide).
      2. Kinds of threats vary from killing to doing serious bodily harm.
      3. From instant to imminent threat.
      4. Measurement of belief regarding threats varies as to objective or subjective.

VI. Intoxication may or may not be a defense.
   A. Voluntary is no excuse.
   B. Involuntary is an excuse.

VII. Entrapment is a defense based on the conduct of the police.
  A. Definition—police inducting someone to commit a crime they wouldn't otherwise commit.
  B. Defense of entrapment is not of constitutional origin.
  C. Subjective test (majority rule)
    1. Did criminal intent originate with the government?
    2. Was the defendant predisposed to commit the crime?
  D. Objective test (minority rule)
    1. Did criminal intent originate with the government?
    2. Would ordinary (reasonable) law-abiding people be tempted to commit the crime?
    3. Dismiss even if the defendant is predisposed.

VIII. Syndrome defenses involve a variety of mental conditions.
  A. Groups of symptoms (syndromes) impair mental capacity
  B. Affects defendant's capacity to form specific intent
  C. Expert testimony is used to inform the jury of the syndrome.

CHAPTER SUMMARY

Defendants who plead excuses admit what they did was wrong but claim they weren't responsible because of mental abnormality or unusual circumstances.

The excuse of insanity is rarely used, is rarely successful, and almost always leads to at least temporary civil commitment if successful. The defense of insanity stands for the proposition that we can't blame people who aren't responsible because of mental diseases or defects that impair their reason or will. Insanity is not the equivalent of mental disease or defect; it is caused by mental disease or defect.

There are a number of tests of the insanity defense. The right-wrong (M'Naghten) test focuses on defects in reason. The product-of-mental illness test (Durham rule) focuses on criminal acts resulting from (are the product of) mental disease. The irresistible impulse test focuses on defects in volition or self-control. The substantial capacity test (Model Penal Code) focuses on reason and self-control. Insanity is an affirmative defense in which the actual burden of proof varies, depending on the jurisdiction.

John Hinckley, who attempted to assassinate President Reagan, was found not guilty by reason of insanity. This verdict troubled many and may have been caused by the fact that the prosecution was required to prove that Hinckley was sane beyond a reasonable doubt. Subsequent federal legislation places the burden on the defendant to prove their insanity by clear and convincing evidence. Some states also changed their law to place the burden of proof on the defendant. The federal government shifted the burden of proof to the defendant by clear and convincing evidence and eliminated any volitional test of insanity.

Diminished capacity involves mental disease or defect that will not qualify for the insanity defense. It may reduce the degree of a crime, because it impairs the capacity to specific intent.

If successful, it may reduce the crime to a lower level or completely acquit because the required *mens rea* cannot be proven. The insanity defense leads to a special verdict.

Age can excuse criminal liability; it can also increase it. At common law, there was an irrebuttable presumption that a child under seven couldn't form criminal intent. Between seven and fourteen, there was a rebuttable presumption of incapacity to form intent. At age fourteen, children were presumed to be capable of forming intent. Many states follow some updated form of the common law. All jurisdictions now have juvenile courts and special laws for juveniles. Juveniles over a certain age who commit serious crimes can be tried in criminal courts as adults.

Duress can be an excuse when individuals are threatened and forced to commit a crime or be killed. In most states, duress is not a defense to murder.

At common law, and in most, if not all states, voluntary intoxication was not a defense. While voluntary intoxication is not an excuse, involuntary intoxication is a defense.

Entrapment occurs when law enforcement officers actively induce, trick or persuade individuals to commit crimes they otherwise wouldn't commit. There are two main types of entrapment defenses. The subjective version focuses on whether or not the defendant was predisposed to commit the crime anyway. The objective version focuses on whether the government action would cause a reasonable, law-abiding person to commit a crime.

Various types of syndromes or conditions such as post-traumatic stress disorder and premenstrual syndrome (PMS) have been tried as defenses. In general, they are not successful.

PRACTICE TEST BANK

Multiple Choice

1. If diminished capacity evidence is utilized in an intentional homicide case, the result of accepting the evidence is _____.
   a. not guilty of any type of homicide
   b. reducing the homicide to a lower degree homicide
   c. not guilty by reason of insanity
   d. a verdict of not guilty by reason of diminished capacity

2. The only states that adopted the ________rule (or product test) for the insanity defense were Maine and New Hampshire.
   a. Durham
   b. M'Naghten
   c. Substantial Capacity
   d. Right-Wrong

3. To establish the duress defense in most jurisdictions, it must be shown that the threat of harm against the defendant was _____.
   a. contingent
   b. foreseeable
   c. overt
   d. reasonably believed to be real

4. In the Substantial Capacity test, the traditional word "know" has been replaced by the word _____.
   a. understand
   b. comprehend
   c. appreciate
   d. aggrandize

5. The objective test of entrapment focuses on government action that _____.
   a. would cause a law-abiding person to commit a crime
   b. provides an opportunity for criminally inclined individuals to commit a crime
   c. would cause a predisposed person to commit a crime
   d. provides an opportunity for a person predisposed to commit a crime

6. Which of the following is not a valid legal excuse for crime?
   a. insanity
   b. involuntary intoxication
   c. entrapment
   d. duress

7. Only the excuse of ________, when raised as a successful defense, does not result in a complete acquittal and immediate release from custody.
   a. entrapment
   b. duress
   c. involuntary intoxication
   d. insanity

8. The M'Naghten test of insanity is referred to as the ________ test.
   a. right-wrong
   b. Durham
   c. McDonough
   d. product

9. The ________ test of insanity deals only with defendants; inability to control their conduct.
   a. product
   b. right-wrong
   c. M'Naghten
   d. irresistible impulse

10. The Model Penal Code's _____ test of insanity incorporates both the cognitive and volitional components of other tests.
   a. Durham
   b. M'Naghten
   c. product
   d. substantial capacity

11. The defense of diminished capacity is available _____.
   a. in most states for most offenses
   b. in most states only when the insanity defense is raised
   c. in most states, but for felonies only
   d. only in few states

12. Most jurisdictions utilize some form of the Model Penal Code's _____ test for their insanity defense.
   a. substantial capacity
   b. Durham
   c. irresistible impulse
   d. product

13. In the 1980's, many states and the federal government changed their _____ defenses after the verdict in the trial of John Hinckley.
   a. duress
   b. diminished capacity
   c. entrapment
   d. insanity

14. The ________ test of insanity incorporates some of the ideas of both the right-wrong and irresistible impulse test.
   a. product
   b Durham
   c. diminished capacity
   d. substantial capacity

15. The defense of diminished capacity _____.
   a. is the same as the right-wrong insanity test
   b. involves a claim that mental illness kept the defendant from having the required intent
   c. asserts that the defendant's acts were involuntary
   d. is always a perfect defense

16. At common law, there was an irrebuttable presumption that children under _____could not form criminal intent.
    a. seven
    b. eight
    c. ten
    d. twelve

17. After the Hinckley insanity verdict, Congress changed the burden of proof for the federal insanity defense. The burden of proof is now on the defendant to prove insanity _____.
    a. by a preponderance of the evidence
    b. beyond a reasonable doubt
    c. by clear and convincing evidence
    d. beyond reasonable suspicion

18. Under the common law, when children reached the age of _____ they were presumed to be capable of criminal intent, just like adults.
    a. seven
    b. twelve
    c. fourteen
    d. seventeen

19. The subjective test of entrapment is an attempt to deal with _____.
    a. organized crime
    b. predisposed criminals
    c. government abuses
    d. young offenders

20 At common law, voluntary intoxication was _____.
    a. a justification
    b. a defense
    c. a mitigating factor
    d. an aggravating factor

21. Combat soldiers and others subjected to extreme situations that later commit crimes sometimes attempt to use the _____ defense.
    a. PMS
    b. post-traumatic stress syndrome
    c. chronic fatigue syndrome
    d. traumatic automaton stress induced

22. The objective test of entrapment is so named because the test revolves around _____.
    a. subjective reactions to police conduct
    b. whether an objectively predisposed person would commit the crime
    c. how a hypothetical, reasonable person would react
    d. public attitudes toward the seriousness of the crime

23. Which of the following would not be a mental disease or defect under the Model Penal Code and in most states for purposes of the insanity defense?
    a. psychopathic or anti-social personality
    b. schizophrenia
    c. psychosis
    d. paranoia

24. Which of the following tests of insanity is totally volitional?
    a. substantial capacity
    b. M'Naghten
    c. Durham
    d. irresistible impulse

25. The M'Naghten test of insanity grew out of M'Naghten's attempt to kill British Prime Minister _____ in 1843.
    a. Edward Drummond
    b. Robert Peel
    c. Thomas Nast
    d. Carl Rogers

26. Excuses tend to involve either _____ people or circumstances.
    a. mitigating
    b. codependent
    c. abnormal
    d. contingent

27. The hypothetical situation of a man who believes he's squeezing lemons but is really strangling his wife to death is an example of the _____ approach to insanity.
    a. subjective
    b. cognitive
    c. volitional
    d. objective

28. Under the Model Penal Code test of insanity, the defendant must lack _____ mental control.
    a. total
    b. complete
    c. partial
    d. substantial

29. Which of the following is an excuse, rather than a justification?
    a. duress
    b. necessity
    c. self-defense
    d. defense of others

30. In a majority of states, the defense of _____ cannot be used to a charge of murder.
    a. entrapment
    b. insanity
    c. duress
    d. involuntary intoxication

True/False

1. The cognition form of the insanity defense deals with the will or ability to control conduct.
    a. true
    b. false

2. Most jurisdictions utilize the subjective test of entrapment.
    a. true
    b. false

3. The irresistible impulse test is a cognitive type of insanity defense.
    a. true
    b. false

4. The Durham version of the insanity defense was first announced in a famous English case in the1843.
    a. true
    b. false

5. Most states use some version of the Model Penal Code substantial capacity test of insanity.
    a. true
    b. false

6. The substantial capacity test has both cognitive and volitional elements.
    a. true
    b. false

7. Most defendants who utilize the insanity defense at trial do so unsuccessfully.
    a. true
    b. false

8. Defendants usually succeed when they argue syndrome defenses such as PMS or post-traumatic stress disorder.
    a. true
    b. false

9. In the criminal law, the insanity defense is a medical concept, not a legal one
   a. true
   b. false

10. In all states and the federal courts, the prosecution must disprove insanity by a preponderance of the evidence.
   a. true
   b. false

11. At common law, voluntary intoxication was a defense.
   a. true
   b. false

12. Involuntary intoxication is a recognized defense in most states
   a. true
   b. false

13. A defendant who succeeds with the diminished capacity defense will automatically be committed to a mental hospital.
   a. true
   b. false

14 At common law, a child under twelve years of age could not be guilty of a criminal offense.
   a. true
   b. false

15. In most states, the defense of duress cannot be used in murder prosecutions.
   a. true
   b. false

16. To have a successful duress defense, the defendant must retreat before using force if it can be done safely.
   a. true
   b. false

17. The predisposition of the defendant to commit the crime is relevant in the subjective test of entrapment.
   a. false
   b. true

18. Current federal statutes use the Durham test of insanity.
   a. true
   b. false

19. A defendant who has prior convictions for similar offenses would probably fare best in a jurisdiction that uses the objective test of entrapment.
    a. true
    b. false

20. England did not have an insanity defense until 1960.
    a. true
    b. false

21. In an excuse, the defendant admits doing the act, but argues that the act was right or justified.
    a. true
    b. false

22. The John Hinckley trial and verdict stimulated considerable change in the law of insanity.
    a. true
    b. false

23. Under the irresistible impulse test, the defendant does not have to be suffering from a mental disease or defect.
    a. true
    b. false

24. A psychosis is a form of mental illness that can qualify for the insanity defense.
    a. true
    b. false

25. Since the late 1980s, most jurisdictions and the federal government have abolished the insanity defense.
    a. true
    b. false

<u>Fill in the blank</u>

1. The defense of ______________________________ is recognized in only a few states.

2. ______________ intoxication is not a defense.

3. The M'Naghten test of insanity is also known as the _________ test.

4. At common law, a child under the age of __________ could not be guilty of a crime.

5. The diminished capacity defense relates to negating the ___________________ element of crimes.

6. The Durham or____________ test of insanity basically asks if the mental illness caused the crime.

7. Under the _____________ test of entrapment, the government cannot introduce evidence of the defendant's prior convictions for similar offenses.

8. If government agents offer inducements to get persons to commit crimes, this could implicate the ____________ defense.

9. To establish the insanity defense, it must be shown that the defendant suffered from a mental disease or ____________.

10. In some states, a defendant who is not insane but is mentally ill may be able to use the defense of __________________________.

11. One form of the insanity test is called the _______________________ test.

12. In federal courts, and in many states, the burden of proof on the insanity defense is on the ____________.

13. At one time, the state of ___________ had the diminished capacity defense but later abolished it because of public hostility.

14. At common law, a child was presumed capable of criminal intent upon reaching the age of _____________.

15. Young offenders are typically dealt with in ___________ court rather than adult criminal court.

Essay

1. Discuss the common law rules on age and criminality and compare it with the current approach.

2. Compare and contrast cognitive, volitional, and mixed tests of insanity.

3. Compare and contrast the insanity and diminished capacity defenses.

4. Compare and contrast the two major approaches to the entrapment defense.

5. Compare and contrast involuntary and voluntary intoxication as defenses to crime.

CHAPTER 8 ANSWER KEY

Multiple Choice

1—b (232) 2—a (244) 3—d (259) 4—c (246) 5—d (252)

6—b (262) 7—d (240) 8—a (242) 9—d (245) 10—d (246)

11—d (252) 12—a (246) 13—d (252) 14—d (246) 15—b (252)

16—a (253) 17—c (252) 18—c (257) 19—b (268) 20—d (262)

21—b (173) 22—c (271) 23—a (247) 24—d (245) 25—b (241)

26—c (239) 27—b (242) 28—d (246) 29—a (255) 30—c (259)

True-False

1—F (241) 2—T (268) 3—F (245) 4—F (244) 5—T (246)

6—T (246) 7—T (240) 8—F (272) 9—F (240) 10—F (252)

11—F (262) 12—T (262) 13—F (253) 14—F (253) 15—T (259)

16—F (259) 17—T (268) 18—F (246) 19—T (268) 20—F (241)

21—F (239) 22—T (246) 23—F (245) 24—T (245) 25—F (252)

Fill in the blank

1—diminished capacity (252) 2—voluntary (262) 3—right-wrong (241) 4—seven (243)

5—*mens rea* (253) 6—product (244) 7—objective (271) 8—entrapment (267)

9—defect (241) 10—diminished capacity (253) 11—irresistible impulse (245)

12—defendant (252) 13—California (253) 14—fourteen (254) 15—juvenile (254)

Chapter 9 Crimes Against Persons I: Criminal Homicide

LEARNING OBJECTIVES

After studying this chapter, students will

1. understand the historical development of the law of homicide.
2. be familiar with the *mens rea* and actus *reus* of various types and degrees of homicide.
3. understand the concept of malice aforethought.
4. be familiar with the concept of implied malice.
5. understand the concept of felony murder.
6. be able to differentiate between first and second degree murder.
7. understand the function of mitigating and aggravating circumstances.
8. be able to differentiate between voluntary and involuntary manslaughter.
9 understand all the elements of voluntary manslaughter.
10. be familiar with all the elements of involuntary manslaughter.
11. understand the misdemeanor-manslaughter and unlawful act-manslaughter doctrines.

KEYWORDS AND CONCEPTS

Justifiable homicide—homicide for which the defendant has a legal justification; p. 283
Excusable homicide—homicide for which the defendant has a legal excuse; 283
Criminal homicide—homicide that is neither excusable nor justifiable; p. 283
Murder—killing with malice aforethought (common law); p. 283
Malice—intentional killing without excuse or justification; p. 283
Aforethought—planning the killing in advance; p. 283
Manslaughter—intentional killing in the heat of passion; p. 283
Depraved-heart murder—unintentional killing during dangerous behavior p. 283
Homicide *actus reus*—causing the death of another person; p. 284
Fetal death statute—creates crime of killing a fetus; p. 285
Brain death—modern medical definition of when life ends; p. 291
Criminal homicide *mens rea*—varies by jurisdiction; includes intentional to negligent; p. 291
Express or implied malice aforethought—form of criminal homicide *mens rea*; p. 292
First-degree murder—most serious form of murder today; p. 292
Premeditation—a deliberate judgment or decision to kill; p. 293
Torture murder—aggravating factor that may warrant death penalty; p. 298
Second-degree murder—generally an unpremeditated but intentional killing; p. 302
Felony murder—unintentional killing during course of committing a felony; p. 304
Third-party exception—not felony murder if third person kills other criminal; p. 305
Resisting-victim exception—exception to the third party exception for felony murder; p. 306
Voluntary manslaughter—intentional killing during heat of passion; p. 315
Adequate provocation—provocation sufficient to qualify killing for voluntary manslaughter; p. 315
Objective test of cooling-off time—would a reasonable person under the same circumstances had time to cool off after the provocation and before the killing; p. 315

Common-law paramour rule—husband who catches wife in act of adultery had adequate provocation to kill and is thus guilty only of voluntary manslaughter; p. 319
Subjective provocation—defendant must have actually felt provoked; p. 322
Reasonable provocation—reasonable person in same situation would have been provoked; p. 322
Involuntary manslaughter—unintentional killing; p. 323
Reckless manslaughter—recklessly taking the life of another; p. 323
Negligent manslaughter—negligently taking the life of another; p. 323
Misdemeanor manslaughter—unintentional killing during commission of misdemeanor; p. 323
Criminal recklessness—conscious creation of serious risk; p. 323
Criminal negligence—unknowing creation of serious risk; p. 323
Gross criminal negligence—another term for criminal negligence; p. 323
Unlawful act manslaughter—unintentional killing during commission of unlawful act; p. 326

CHAPTER OUTLINE

I. To understand criminal homicide law, one must understand its history.
- A. Since the 1700's, the law has recognized three kinds of homicide: justifiable, excusable, and criminal.
- B. Criminal homicide is the most serious of all felonies known to our law.
- C. Criminal homicide is divided into two categories: murder and manslaughter.

II. The elements of criminal homicide are act, intent, concurrence, causation and harm.
- A. *Actus reus*—taking the life of or causing the death of another person (live human being)
    - 1. Depends on legal definition of:
        - a. When life begins
        - b. When life ends
    - 2. Defining the beginning and end of life is controversial and differs among jurisdictions (some include fetal murder and brain death).
- B. *Mens rea*—varies over time and from jurisdiction. Typically:
    - 1. Purposely (intentionally)
    - 2. Knowingly
    - 3. Recklessly
    - 4. Negligently
- C. Causation—acts that set in motion a chain of events that amount to cause in fact or legal cause of the death of another.
- D. Criminal harm resulting in the death of another

III. Murder is the most serious form of criminal homicide.
- A. At common law, murder was the unlawful killing of another with malice aforethought.
- B. Historically, the concept of "malice aforethought" was expanded to include implied malice. It consisted of five mental states—the specific intent to do one of the following:
    - 1. Kill another person

2. Seriously injure another person
3. Commit specified dangerous felonies
4. Forcibly resist a lawful arrest
5. Create a higher than criminally reckless risk of death or serious bodily injury (depraved-heart murder)

C. Today, most jurisdictions have four types of murder:
1. First-degree murder (capital offense in states with the death penalty)
    a. Premeditated, deliberate killings
    b. Atrocious, brutal, or cruel murders (in capital cases)
2. Second-degree murder
    a. Intentional killing without premeditation
    b. Killings resulting from the intent to do serious bodily injury
    c. Killings resulting from the resisting of lawful arrest
    d. Killings that occur during the commission of felonies
3. Felony murder—unintentional death that occurs while committing dangerous felonies
    a. Intent to commit the underlying crime satisfies the mens rea of felony murder.
    b. Felony murder has three goals:
        (1) Deterrence
        (2) Reduce violence
        (3) Punish wrongdoers
    c. Four states have abolished it.
    d. When someone besides the defendant caused the death
        (1) Third-party exception prevents felony murder conviction.
        (2) Resisting victim exception allows felony murder conviction.
4. Corporation murders
    a. Corporations can legally commit murder.
    b. Usually, prosecutions of corporations for criminal homicide don't succeed.

IV. Manslaughter is divided into two types—voluntary and involuntary.

A. Two types: voluntary or involuntary

B. Elements of voluntary manslaughter
1. *Actus reus*—taking the life or causing the death of another person
2. *Mens rea*—intent to kill or cause serious bodily harm
3. Adequate provocation
    a. Is a circumstance element.
    b. Occurs in the sudden heat of passion before there was a reasonable time for the passion to cool off
    c. Caused both the passion and the killing
    d. Is specified by law
        (1) Fighting (mutual combat)
        (2) Assault and battery
        (3) Trespass
        (4) Adultery (paramour rule)
    e. Response must be reasonable to ordinary people.

f. Never consists of words

4. Causation—the acts that triggered the chain of events that led to the death
5. Result—the death of another

C. Involuntary manslaughter is the killing of another person unintentionally.

1. Requires the mens rea of either criminal recklessness or criminal negligence
2. Occurs during the commission of unlawful acts (like reckless or negligent driving)
3. Most jurisdictions no longer recognize the misdemeanor-manslaughter or unlawful act manslaughter doctrines.

CHAPTER SUMMARY

Criminal homicides are different from all other crimes because of the finality of the result—the death of the victim. Because of the seriousness of the harm and the penalty, this is probably the most complex area of substantive criminal law. Although the definitions vary from state to state there are many common principles. All criminal homicides involve the killing of another person. The *mens rea* can include knowingly, intentionally, purposely, recklessly and negligently. The *mens rea* must trigger the act and the act must cause the death. The causation element has two components: cause in fact and legal cause.

The law of homicide has its origins in the common law. Early on, there were only three types of homicide: justifiable, excusable and criminal. A justifiable murder was not punishable if the defendant could establish a justification such as self-defense. An excusable murder was not criminal if the defendant could establish an excuse such as an accident.

Murder was defined as killing with malice aforethought. The crime of murder was expanded by creating implied malice situations, such as the deprave heart and felony murder. The common law also created the crime of voluntary manslaughter, which involved an intentional killing during the heat of passion.

The *actus reus* of criminal homicide is killing another person. Today, in many jurisdictions, a fetus can be the victim of a criminal homicide. Advances in medical science have changed the definition of death. Brain death qualifies as death even though the person may be able to continue breathing.

The *mens rea* of criminal homicide is typically intentionally, knowingly, recklessly, or negligently (criminal negligence). There are, however, other types of murders. For instance, the intent to commit a qualifying felony substitutes for the intent to kill in felony murder. Many states have limited the felony murder doctrine to violent or dangerous felonies

Most of the law of criminal homicide is about grading the offense according to the elements of *mens rea*, *actus reus*, or mitigating or aggravating circumstances. The common law did not recognize degrees of murder. Pennsylvania was the first state to divide murder into two degrees. Most states have four basic types of murder: first-degree murder, second-degree murder, voluntary manslaughter and involuntary manslaughter. Grading murder into first and second degree is important because in some states only first-degree (or capital) murders qualify for the death penalty (or prison for life without parole in states without the death penalty). Second-degree murder is typically an unpremeditated but intentional killing.

Most murder statutes apply to corporations. However, in most cases, liability doesn't extend beyond the rare prosecution for involuntary manslaughter in outrageous cases.

A voluntary manslaughter is an intentional, sudden killing triggered by an adequate provocation. Provocation isn't an excuse for criminal homicide; it only reduces the punishment to allow for human weaknesses. Most jurisdictions have both objective and subjective requirements for the elements of voluntary manslaughter. Only certain types of provocation are deemed legally adequate. Usually these are mutual combat, assault and battery, trespass and adultery. Words alone are almost never deemed an adequate provocation. Catching a spouse in the act of adultery is generally recognized as an adequate provocation. Further, the killer must not have cooled off from the sudden passion. If the killer did cool off, it is an intentional murder and not a voluntary manslaughter. Specifically, the elements of voluntary manslaughter are as follows. The *actus reus* is killing of another person. The *mens rea* is intent to kill or inflict serious bodily injury. The circumstances are sudden heat of passion flowing from an adequate provocation (or honest but unreasonable belief that killing was necessary in self-defense). The acts must cause the death of another.

Involuntary manslaughter is the least blameworthy form of criminal homicide. It involves unintentional (reckless or negligent) killing. Recklessness involves conscious creation of a serous and unjustifiable risk. Negligence involves unknowing creation of a substantial and unjustifiable risk.

The common law and early statutes recognized a form of involuntary manslaughter that involved an intentional killing during the course of committing a misdemeanor or an unlawful act. Most jurisdictions have severely limited or abolished this form of involuntary manslaughter.

PRACTICE TEST BANK

Multiple Choice

1. Most states have _____.
    a. abolished felony murder
    b. limited the types of felonies which qualify to violent or dangerous felonies
    c. made felony murder a form of involuntary manslaughter
    d. made felony murder a form of voluntary manslaughter

2. Implied malice includes intent to _____.
    a. commit any felony or misdemeanor
    b. commit a dangerous misdemeanor
    c. commit any illegal act
    d. inflict serious bodily harm

3. The degree of murder or type of homicide is determined by the *actus reus*, special circumstances and the _____.
   a. concurrence
   b. act
   c. harm
   d. *mens rea*

4. The term "homicide" is usually defined as _____.
   a. killing another live human being
   b. a criminal offense where the victim dies
   c. a murder or a suicide
   d. a murder

5. A murder that was perpetrated by means of planned, intentional poisoning of two elderly parents to collect life insurance would be a _____.
   a. second degree murder
   b. voluntary manslaughter
   c. first degree murder
   d. voluntary manslaughter

6. An unintentional criminal homicide that resulted from a conscious risk of harm greater than recklessness, is usually termed a _____.
   a. felony murder
   b. depraved heart murder
   c. voluntary manslaughter
   d. excusable homicide

7. With regard to cooling off for voluntary manslaughter, assuming the defendant did, in fact, honestly not cool off, most courts would also then apply a/n ________ reasonable person test.
   a. objective
   b. overt
   c. lenient
   d. subjective

8. Although it is no longer the case, a few states went further than most with the paramour rule. In these states, wife killings during adultery were _____.
   a. justifiable homicides
   b. voluntary manslaughter
   c. involuntary manslaughter
   d. depraved-heart murders

9. Originally, the benefit of the paramour rule could be claimed by _____.
   a. wives only
   b. both husbands and wives
   c. the spouse's paramour only
   d. husbands only

10. Conscious creation of a substantial and unjustifiable risk is _____.
   a. negligence
   b. gross negligence
   c. recklessness
   d. criminal negligence

11. If the defendant accidentally killed the store clerk during an armed robbery this would be _____.
   a. felony murder
   b. excusable homicide
   c. Involuntary manslaughter
   d depraved heart murder

12. Common law judges expanded the original definition of murder by creating the concept of ________ malice aforethought.
   a. express
   b. constitutive
   c. implied
   d. latent

13. At early common law, at first there was only one type of criminal homicide, homicide _____.
   a. committed during a felony
   b. that was neither excused nor justified
   c. depraved heart murder
   d. in the form of manslaughter

14. As the common law developed, murder was distinguished from manslaughter in that murder required _____.
   a. malice aforethought
   b. adequate provocation
   c. heat of passion
   d. no *actus reus*

15. In 1794, ________ was the first state to separate murder into two degrees.
   a. Virginia
   b. New York
   c. Pennsylvania
   d. Massachusetts

16. As compared to traditional murder law, the felony murder rule doesn't require _____.
    a. malice aforethought or an intent or purpose to kill
    b. intent to commit a felony
    c. an *actus reus*
    d. that the defendant's acts cause the victim's death

17. The common law crime of manslaughter was eventually divided into two separate types, _____.
    a. voluntary and involuntary
    b. deliberate and premeditated
    c. first and second degree
    d. with implied or express malice

18. The main difference between voluntary and involuntary manslaughter is that in involuntary manslaughter the killing is _____.
    a. unintentional
    b. totally unforeseeable
    c. with implied malice
    d. with express malice

19. If the defendant killed another in an honest but unreasonable belief that the killing was necessary for self-defense, this would be the crime of _____.
    a. involuntary manslaughter
    b. voluntary manslaughter
    c. excusable homicide
    d. justifiable homicide

20. Voluntary manslaughter involves intentionally killing another in the sudden heat of passion which _____.
    a. was caused by a legally recognized adequate provocation
    b. was caused by a mental disease or defect
    c. caused the actor to be reckless
    d. gave the actor time to cool off

21. Which of the following is not deemed to be a legally adequate provocation for voluntary manslaughter?
    a. verbal provocation
    b. mutual combat
    c. adultery by spouse
    d. assault and battery

22. The *mens rea* of involuntary manslaughter is usually _____.
    a. recklessly or negligently
    b. intentionally
    c. deliberate and premeditated
    d. implied malice

23. Which of the following is typically an aggravating circumstance that will justify infliction of the death penalty?
    a. torture of victim
    b. victim attempted to defend themselves
    c. victim was related to offender
    d. victim was a stranger

24. Over time, the substantive law of criminal homicide has _____.
    a. become more complex
    b. come to exclude corporations from liability for criminal homicide
    c. come to include more capital offenses
    d. allowed numerous blameworthy individuals to avoid punishment

25. Unlawful act manslaughter is sometimes also referred to as _____.
    a. voluntary manslaughter
    b. misdemeanor manslaughter
    c. felony murder
    d. depraved heart murder

26. The _____ element of all homicides is the killing of another person.
    a. *mens rea*
    b. *actus reus*
    c. circumstances
    d. concurrence

27. In the first statute creating two degrees of murder (1794), (and in some current statutes), second degree murder was defined as _____.
    a. a deliberate and premeditated killing
    b. a killing with malice aforethought
    c. intentional killing during the course of rape, robbery, etc.
    d. any murder that is not a first degree murder

28. Felony murder requires intent _____.
    a. to kill
    b. to inflict serious bodily injury
    c. to inflict any bodily injury
    d. to commit a felony

29. Felony murders are usually _____.
    a. first or second degree murders
    b. second degree murders or voluntary manslaughters
    c. voluntary or involuntary manslaughters
    d. involuntary manslaughters or negligent homicides

30. In most jurisdictions, second-degree murder is a murder _____.
   a. with malice aforethought
   b. done intentionally but without premeditation
   c. done with premeditation but not intentionally
   d. done with recklessness aforethought

True-False

1. Second degree murder is generally an intentional but unpremeditated murder.
   a. true
   b. false

2. No corporation has ever been charged with a criminal homicide.
   a. true
   b. false

3. A defendant who cools off after the provocation and then intentionally kills is guilty of voluntary manslaughter.
   a. true
   b. false

4. Reckless or negligent criminal homicides are usually termed involuntary manslaughter.
   a. true
   b. false

5. Recklessness has both objective and subjective components.
   a. true
   b. false

6. At common law, murder was divided into first, second, and third degrees.
   a. true
   b. false

7. In some jurisdictions, murders that include aggravating circumstances (torture, heinous, atrocious, or cruel) are capital offenses.
   a. true
   b. false

8. The Eighth Amendment requires case-by-case consideration of aggravating and mitigating factors before the death penalty can be imposed.
   a. true
   b. false

9. Manslaughter was not common law crime.
   a. true
   b. false

10. Insulting gestures or words and racial slurs are adequate legal provocation for manslaughter.
    a. true
    b. false

11. At common law, a criminal homicide committed with malice aforethought is a murder.
    a. true
    b. false

12. All felony murders are intentional homicides.
    a. true
    b. false

13. Not all homicides are criminal.
    a. true
    b. false

14. Corporations cannot be guilty of criminal homicide.
    a. true
    b. false

15. Voluntary manslaughter is a form of unintentional homicide.
    a. true
    b. false

16. The trend in the law is to expand the illegal act-manslaughter rule.
    a. true
    b. false

17. In most jurisdictions today, any type of felony will qualify for the felony murder rule.
    a. true
    b. false

18. Most, if not all, jurisdictions recognize brain death as a legal death.
    a. true
    b. false

19. An accidental killing involving no fault on the actor's part would be an excusable homicide.
    a. true
    b. false

20. In some states, a person can be guilty of the crime of killing a fetus.
    a. true
    b. false

21. A homicide committed in valid self-defense would be a justifiable homicide.
    a. true
    b. false

22. The common law term "aforethought" refers to planning in advance.
    a. true
    b. false

23. The *actus reus* of homicide is killing another person or human being.
    a. true
    b. false

24. Most, if not all, involuntary manslaughters have two *actus reus* elements.
    a. true
    b. false

25. At common law, life (or becoming a person) began at conception.
    a. true
    b. false

<u>Fill in the blank</u>

1. For a felony to qualify for the felony murder rule, most states require that the felony be a violent or ________________ felony.

2. One of the most highly publicized cases of alleged corporate criminal homicides involved the _________________ automobile.

3. A valid self-defense killing is a form of ____________ homicide.

4. At common law, murder was killing someone with ____________.

5. Insulting gestures and words are not legally adequate provocation for purposes of ____________ manslaughter.

6. An accidental killing can be a murder and not an excusable homicide under the ____________ murder rule.

7. The *mens rea* for involuntary manslaughter is recklessness or ____________.

8. The unintentional killing form of manslaughter is ____________ manslaughter.

9. An intentional killing that occurred under circumstances of imperfect self-defense is a _____________ manslaughter.

10. The ________________________ rule is an exception to the felony murder rule.

11. A killing is with ____________ if it is intentional and without excuse or justification.

12. The most serious form of murder today is capital or ___________________ murder.

13. Conscious creation of a serious and substantial risk is called ____________.

14. Creating serious and substantial risks, but not being aware of it, is called ____________.

15. An unintentional death caused by driving while intoxicated would be a form of ____________ manslaughter.

<u>Essay</u>

1. Discuss the development of homicide under the common law.

2. Compare and contrast reckless and negligent involuntary manslaughter.

3. Compare and contrast voluntary and involuntary manslaughter.

4. Compare and contrast justifiable, excusable, and criminal homicide.

5. Define and discuss the four main types of criminal homicide found in most states.

CHAPTER 9 ANSWER KEY

Multiple Choice

1—b (304)	2—d (292)	3—d (291)	4—a (284)	5—c (293)
6—b (283)	7—a (315)	8—a (319)	9—d (319)	10—c (323)
11—a (304)	12—c (292)	13—b (283)	14—a (315)	15—c (292)
16—a (304)	17—a (315)	18—a (323)	19—b (315)	20—a (285)
21—a (283)	22—a (323)	23—a (298)	24—a (283)	25—b (326)
26—b (324)	27—d (292)	28—d (305)	29—a (304)	30—b (302)

True-False

1—T (302)	2—F (311)	3—F (315)	4—T (323)	5—T (323)
6—F (283)	7—T (298)	8—T (293	9—F (314)	10—F (315)
11—T (283)	12—F (304)	13—T (283)	14—F (310)	15—F (315)
16—F (326)	17—F (304)	18—T (291)	19—T (283)	20—T (285)
21—T (283)	22—T (283)	23—T (284)	24—F (292)	25—F (284)

Fill in the blank

1—dangerous (304)	2—Ford Pinto (310)	3—justifiable (283)	4--malice (283)
5—voluntary (315)	6—felony (304)	7—negligence (323)	8—involuntary (323)
9—voluntary (315)	10—third party exception (305)		11—malice (283)
12—first degree (292)	13—recklessness (323)	14—negligence (323)	15—involuntary (324)

Chapter 10 Crimes Against Persons II: Criminal Sexual Conduct, Bodily Injury and Personal Restraint

LEARNING OBJECTIVES

After studying this chapter, students will

1. understand the traditional and common law approaches to rape.
2. be familiar with modern changes in the law of rape and rape prosecutions.
3. understand the controversy about whether rape is or is not a specific intent crime.
4. know the basics of the crime of statutory rape and the mistake of age defense.
5. know the traditional difference between assault and battery.
6. understand the current approach to assault and battery.
7. be familiar with the crime of kidnapping.
8. be familiar with crime of false imprisonment.
9. know the difference between kidnapping and false imprisonment.

KEY TERMS AND CONCEPTS

Battery—unwanted and unjustified touching of another person; p. 333
Common-law rape—intentional forced heterosexual vaginal penetration; p. 333
Common law sodomy—anal intercourse between two males; p. 334
Criminal sexual conduct statutes—modern broad approach to sex crimes; p. 334
Aggravated rape—rape by strangers with weapons or with physical injury; p. 334
Unarmed acquaintance rape—non-consensual sex between acquaintances; p. 334
Element of consent—main focus of law of rape until 1970s; p. 336
Utmost resistance standard—required maximum resistance by victim; p. 336
Reasonable resistance standard—modern approach to rape victim resistance; p. 337
Corroboration rule—old rule that required corroboration of rape victim testimony; p. 337
Rape shield statutes—modern statutes designed to protect rape victims; p. 337
Prompt reporting rule—old rule requiring that rape victims report rape promptly; p. 337
Marital rape exception—old rule that a man could not rape his wife; p. 337
Sexual penetration—modern approach to rape includes any form of sexual penetration; p. 338
Criminal sexual contact—crime of offensive sexual touching; p. 338
Rape *actus reus*—two of these, sexual penetration and force/threat of force; p. 339
Extrinsic force standard—requires force in addition to force of penetration; p. 339
Intrinsic force standard—requires only the force of penetration; p. 339
Specific-intent rape—must intend to have intercourse without consent; p. 345
Statutory rape—consensual sex with young victim; p. 349
Defense of reasonable mistake of victim's age–may or may not be available in statutory rape cases; p. 349
Simple rape (second degree)—basic rape without any aggravating circumstances; p. 353
Aggravated rape (first degree)—rape with circumstances that enhance punishment; p. 353
Assault—attempted or threatened battery; p. 353
Attempted battery assault—specific intent to commit battery and substantial but unsuccessful steps to complete battery; p. 355
Threatened battery assault—intentional scaring without a battery; p. 355

Intentional scaring—another term for threatened battery assault; p. 355
Stalking—intentionally scaring by following, harassing, etc.; p. 355
Right of locomotion—right to move about and come and go as we please; p. 362
Kidnapping—illegally seizing, carrying away and confining another; p. 362
Asportation requirement—element of kidnapping requiring that the victim be moved or carried away; p. 364
False imprisonment—unlawfully compelling a person to remain where they do not wish to remain or to go where they do not wish to go; p. 367

CHAPTER OUTLINE

I. Other than homicide, there are three kinds of crimes against persons--sexual, bodily injury and restraint.
- A. Sex offenses (*e.g.*, rape)
- B. Bodily injury crimes (*e.g.*, assault)
- C. Personal restraint crimes (*e. g.* kidnapping

II. Forcible rape was an offense at common law but has been modified greatly since then.
- A. The history of rape law
    - 1. Originally, only narrowly defined rape and sodomy
        - a. Rape—forced heterosexual vaginal penetration of a woman not married to the rapist
        - b. Sodomy—anal intercourse between males
    - 2. The elements of common-law rape
        - a. Intentional vaginal intercourse
        - b. Between a man with a woman not his wife
        - c. Achieved by force or threat of serious bodily harm
        - d. Without the woman's consent
    - 3. Victims could testify against rapists, but the woman's credibility depended on three conditions that were difficult (if not impossible) to prove:
        - a. Her chastity
        - b. Whether she reported the rape promptly
        - c. Whether the rape was corroborated by other testimony
    - 4. Force and resistance standard—focused on the woman's consent
        - a. Utmost resistance standard (1600s–1950s)—victims had to prove by resistance to the utmost they didn't consent.
        - b. Reasonable resistance standard (1950s–1970s)—amount of required resistance depended on the circumstances of each case.
    - 5. Rape and related sex offense law reforms (1970s–1980s)
        - a. Changes in prosecution procedures
            - (1) Abolished the corroboration rule
            - (2) Relaxed the prompt reporting rule
            - (3) Banned introduction of evidence of the victim's past sexual conduct through rape shield laws
        - b. Changes in the definition of rape and related sex offenses

(1) Marital rape exception (husbands can't rape wives) abolished in some states.
(2) Consolidated criminal sexual conduct statutes
    (a) All nonconsensual sexual penetrations and contacts included.
    (b) Sex offenses made gender-neutral
    (c) Seriousness of offense divided into several degrees, graded by:
        i. Penetration (more serious) and contact (less serious)
        ii. Use of force (more serious)
        iii. Physical injury aggravates crime

B. The elements of modern rape law
   1. Rape *actus reus*, two parts
      a. Sexual penetration, however slight
      b. By force or threat of force
         (1) "Intrinsic" in some jurisdictions—only the amount of physical exertion to achieve penetration in nonconsensual sex needed.
         (2) "Extrinsic" in some jurisdictions—some force in addition to the amount of exertion to achieve nonconsensual penetration needed.
      c. No force or threat required if victim is insane or tricked.
   2. Rape *mens rea*
      a. English rule—specific intent to penetrate with force without consent
      b. Maine rule—strict liability with respect to intent to use force
      c. Middle rule—recklessness or negligence regarding penetration without consent
   3. Circumstance—nonconsent by the victim
      a. Formal law—state has to prove nonconsent beyond a reasonable doubt.
      b. Informal practice—defendants raise consent by the victim as a defense.
      c. Consent doesn't have to be in writing.

C. Statutory rape
   1. Victim's immaturity substitutes for the element of consent.
   2. Strict liability as to age in most states
   3. A few states allow a defense of reasonable mistake of age.

III. Bodily injury crimes involve offensive touching or bodily harm.

A. Battery is unwanted and unjustified offensive touching; assault is either an attempted or threatened battery.

B. The elements of battery
   1. *Actus reus*
      a. Unlawful touching
      b. Only unauthorized offensive touching (parents and law enforcement officers are authorized)

2. *Mens rea* varies as to whether it requires purposely, knowingly, recklessly, or negligently offensive touching.

C. Grading the seriousness depends on:
1. The degree of injury—mere touching, minor injury, or serious injury.
2. The circumstances of the touching—like injuries caused by loose dogs or drug abuse.

D. The elements of assault
1. Assault requires no touching
2. Kinds:
    a. Attempted battery elements—having the specific intent to commit battery and taking steps to complete it.
    b. Threatened battery elements—intentionally scaring the victim
3. Victim awareness
    a. Not important in attempted battery because the offense focuses on the physical injury.
    b. Indispensable in threatened battery because the offense focuses on fear of the victim.

E. The Model assault and battery statute
1. Part of the Model Penal Code
2. Integrates, rationalizes, and grades assault and battery
3. Takes into account *actus reus*, *mens rea*, circumstance elements, and criminal harm

IV. Kidnapping and false imprisonment are the primary personal restraint crimes.

A. Laws protect the fundamental right of locomotion—the right to move about and come and go as we please.

B. Kidnapping
1. Elements of common-law kidnapping:
    a. Seizing, carrying away (asportation of), and confining another person
    b. By force or threat of force, fraud, or deception
    c. Intent to deprive the other person of her or his liberty
2. Elements of modern kidnapping law
    a. *Actus reus*—asportation requirement recognizes even practically no movement of the victim.
    b. *Mens rea*—the specific intent to confine, significantly restrain, or hold victims in secret without the victim's consent.
    c. Aggravating circumstances include kidnapping for the purpose of:
        (1) Sexual invasion
        (2) Obtaining a hostage
        (3) Obtaining ransom
        (4) Robbing the victim
        (5) Murdering the victim
        (6) Blackmail
        (7) Terrorizing the victim
        (8) Achieving political aims
3. Grading the seriousness of kidnapping

a. Simple
b. Aggravated

C. False imprisonment
1. *Actus reus*—keeping another person from moving freely (no asportation requirement)
2. *Mens rea*—having the specific intent to confine or restrain another person without their consent

CHAPTER SUMMARY

Crimes against persons involve four types: taking a life (homicide), unwanted sexual invasions (rape and sex offenses), bodily injury (assault and battery), and personal restraint (kidnapping, false imprisonment). In one form or another, all of these were common law crimes.

Sex offenses are serious even if there is no physical injury, because they violate intimacy and privacy and bodily integrity in a way typical physical injuries cannot. The criminal justice system handles rapes by strangers and men with weapons well, but it doesn't do as well with the overwhelming number of rapes by men who know their victims, including date rape.

The old rape law defined a crime of forcible sexual penetration that only men could commit against women who weren't their wives. The elements of rape at common law were:1. intentional vaginal intercourse, 2. between a man and a woman who was not his wife, 3. achieved by force or a threat of severe bodily harm, 4. without the woman's consent

Modern statutes have expanded the crime of rape and other sex crimes in criminal sexual conduct statutes. These new offenses include a list of gender-neutral sex offenses, involving unwanted sexual penetrations and contacts. Rape in most jurisdictions today has four elements: 1. the *actus reus* of sexual penetration, 2. the *actus reus* of force, or threat of force, to accomplish sexual penetration (or some substitute such as unconsciousness, mental impairment, etc.), 3. the *mens rea* of intentional sexual penetration, and 4. the circumstance of the lack of victim consent.

One controversial issue is whether there should also be a specific intent element in rape. The leading case on the point is the controversial English case of Regina v. Morgan (1975). Morgan and three companions were drinking in a bar. When they failed to find female companionship, Morgan invited the others to come home with him to have sexual intercourse with his wife. Morgan told the others that she would want to have sex with them, and would only pretend to resist. He told them not to worry if she struggled because she liked rough sex. The Sixth House of Lords (England's highest court) overturned the convictions because the defendants didn't specifically intend to have sexual intercourse without the victim's consent. Why? Because they believed that Morgan's wife wanted sex and wanted the struggle.

When American courts face that intent question, they vary in their response. Many come down between the English specific-intent rule and strict liability on the issue of intent or knowledge to have sex without the victims consent. Some of these courts have adopted a reckless or negligent standard with regard to the consent problem.

Current rape law has shifted the emphasis from the resistance of victims to lack of consent. The traditional emphasis on physical violence (or threats thereof) to satisfy the element of force in the *actus reus* of rape is shifting in modern rape law to the sufficiency of nonconsent to unwanted sexual activity.

According to the law, the prosecution has to prove nonconsent by the victim beyond a reasonable doubt. However, as a matter of strategy, defendants claim victim consent as a defense.

Most current statutes divide rape into two degrees: simple (second-degree) rape and aggravated (first-degree) rape. Aggravated rape involves at least one of the following circumstances: victim suffers serious bodily injury, stranger rape, rape occurs in conjunction with another crime, rapist is armed, multiple offenders, or victim is a minor while the rapist is significantly older. All other rapes are "simple" rapes with lesser penalties.

Much of the law of rape and rape prosecutions has changed over the years. The marital exception and prompt report rule have been abolished in many jurisdictions. Corroboration of the victim's testimony is no longer required. Rape shield laws limit the ability of the defense to bring out evidence of the victim's prior sex life. Utmost resistance by the victim is no longer required. Reasonable resistance is enough.

Bodily injury crimes include unlawful nonsexual contacts (battery) or threats of them (assault). The elements of battery are negligently, recklessly, knowingly or purposely causing and unlawful, offensive touching of another. The grading of the seriousness of a battery depends on the amount of injury and the circumstances of the touching.

An assault requires no touching. There are two kinds of assault: attempted battery (having the specific intent to commit battery and taking steps to complete it), and threatened battery (intentionally scaring the victim). In both types, the victim must be aware of the defendant's conduct.

Kidnapping and false imprisonment are crimes against the right to come and go as we please. At common law, kidnapping consisted of six elements: 1. Seizing, 2. Carrying away (asportation of) and 3. Confining 4. Another person 5. By force, threat of force, fraud, or deception 6. With the intent to deprive the other of their liberty.

The critical difference between false imprisonment and kidnapping is that the *actus reus* of asportation (carrying away) of victims is required in kidnapping. Modern interpretations have rendered the asportation requirement of kidnapping almost meaningless

Kidnapping is usually divided into two degrees: simple and aggravated. The most common aggravating circumstances include kidnapping for the purpose of: sexual invasion, taking a hostage, getting ransom, terrorizing the victim, and achieving political goals. The penalty for aggravated kidnapping is typically life imprisonment and, until recently, even death.

The elements of false imprisonment are: restraining another person's liberty, with specific intent to restrain. The Model Penal Code requires the restraint to "interfere substantially with the victim's liberty," but in most states, any interference with another person's liberty suffices. In many states false imprisonment means forcibly, by threat, or secretly confining, abducting, imprisoning, or restraining another person against their will and without legal authority.

PRACTICE TEST BANK

Multiple Choice

1. Asportation is an element of kidnapping. Asportation refers to _____.
   a. confining
   b. alleviating
   c. carrying away
   d. restraining

2. The crime of kidnapping has _____ *mens rea* element(s).
   a. no
   b. one
   c. two
   d. three

3. False imprisonment and kidnapping are _____ crimes.
   a. specific intent
   b. strict liability
   c. *mala prohibita*
   d. inchoate

4. The *actus reus* of false imprisonment is _____.
   a. carrying away
   b. threats
   c. abducting
   d. restraint

5. One difference between false imprisonment and kidnapping is that false imprisonment _____.
   a. is a felony
   b. is a strict liability crime
   c. has no asportation element
   d. has only one *actus reus*

6. Prior to recent reforms, proof of lack of consent in rape prosecutions ____.
   a. was irrelevant to the crime of rape
   b. could be established by verbal resistance alone
   c. required proof of physical resistance
   d. required that the defendant show physical signs of being forcibly resisted

7. A battery is an unlawful _____.
   a. attempted assault.
   b. felony
   c. aggravated assault
   d. offensive touching of another

8. Modern assault and/or battery statutes often _____.
   a. have made them capital offenses
   b. have negligence and recklessness as a *mens rea*
   c have made them strict liability crimes
   d. have eliminated purposeful as a *mens rea*

9. The extrinsic force standard of rape requires that the rapist have _____.
   a. used only the force necessary to accomplish the penetration itself
   b. used force beyond that necessary to penetrate the victim
   c. have used only a reasonable amount of force to accomplish the penetration itself
   d. used only reasonable force to overcome the victim's resistance

10. In Regina v. Morgan, Britain's highest court held that the defendants were not guilty of rape because _____.
   a. they reasonably believed the victim was old enough to give valid consent
   b. did not use force on the victim
   c. they reasonably believe the victim consented
   d. the statute had no specific intent requirement

11. In statutory rape cases, the rule in most states is that _____.
   a. there is a defense that the victim was promiscuous
   b. a reasonable mistake as to consent is a defense
   c. there is no *mens rea* in the crime
   d. there is no mistake-of-age defense

12. Under the common law, _____.
   a. there were only two sex crimes, rape and sodomy
   b. there were no sex crimes
   c. rape was the only sex crime
   d. sodomy was the only sex crime

13. In the 1950s, courts began to relax the traditional _____ victim resistance standard and replaced it with a reasonable resistance standard for rape victims.
    a. maximum
    b. utmost
    c. contingent
    d. foreseeable

14. Rape shield statutes _____.
    a. limit evidence of the victim's reputation or past sexual conduct
    b. shield the victim from the media
    c. prohibit cross examination of the rape victim
    d. protect the defendant from prejudicial pretrial publicity

15. In many jurisdictions today, rape statutes have modified the common law by _____.
    a. excluding any defense of victim consent
    b. making rape a capital felony
    c. making the offense gender neutral
    d. eliminating the martial exception

16. Many states now have an offense called felonious or________ assault which is an assault plus other elements such as causing serious bodily injury, using a deadly weapon, or assaulting a peace officer.
    a. grand
    b. aggravated
    c. mitigated
    d. serious.

17. The Model Penal Code is different from both the common law and many state statutes in that the Model Penal Code definition of simple assault _____.
    a. has no offensive touching *actus reus*
    b. provides that assault can be committed vicariously
    c. makes assault a strict liability crime
    d. has no *actus reus* element

18. The offense of ________ rape involves an adult having sex with a child, even if the child consents.
    a. child indecency
    b. criminal contact
    c. statutory
    d. minority

19. Traditionally, all assaults were _____.
    a. felonies
    b. *mala prohibita*
    c. misdemeanors
    d. strict liability crimes

20. In common law rape trials, the victims must have _____ in order to get a conviction.
 a. reported the rape promptly
 b. been unmarried
 c. been over the age of fourteen
 d. been under the age of twelve

21. The crime of rape generally _____.
 a. requires that actual extrinsic force be used against the victim
 b. includes threats of imminent force
 c. has no circumstance element
 d. has no *actus reus* element

22. In many modern rape, sexual assault and criminal sexual conduct statutes, such as that in Minnesota, _____.
 a. a female could be guilty of a penetration crime
 b. the marital exception is retained
 c. the corroboration requirement is retained
 d. have only one degree of offense

23. In most statutes today, _____.
 a. the formerly separate offenses of assault and battery are combined
 b. all assaults are felonies
 c. all batteries are misdemeanors
 d. the common law offenses of battery and aggravated assault are combined

24. Offensive physical contact of another is _____.
 a. always criminal
 b. the *actus reus* of battery
 c. the *actus reus* of assault
 d. the *mens rea* of mayhem

25. Intentionally spitting in someone's face to insult them _____.
 a. cannot be a crime
 b. could be an assault
 c. can be a battery
 d. can be an aggravated assault

26. If a person's dog attacks and injures a victim, the person _____.
 a. cannot be guilty of any crime unless the person intended that the victim be injured
 b. can only be sued civilly by the victim. There is no crime.
 c. is guilty of battery only if the victim provoked the animal
 d. can be guilty of an assault or battery

27. Intentionally and repeatedly following a person to scare or harass them is usually referred to as the crime of _____.
    a. intimidation
    b. stalking
    c. terroristic threats
    d. habitual harassment

28. The societal value offended by kidnapping and false imprisonment is personal _____.
    a. privacy
    b. solitude
    c. liberty
    d. integrity

29. Kidnapping can be committed by force, threat of force, and _____.
    a. confounding or compounding
    b. mendacity or veracity
    c. fraud or deception
    d. culpability and mendacity

30. Perhaps the most famous kidnapping cases of the 1970s involved the kidnapping of heiress _____.
    a. Paula Lindbergh
    b. Pat Hauptman
    c. Patricia Hearst
    d. Priscilla Lowry

<u>True-False</u>

1. In the Model Penal Code and most states, simple assault is a felony.
    a. true
    b. false

2. At common law, the offense of kidnapping had seven elements.
    a. true
    b. false

3. The crimes of kidnapping and false imprisonment are specific intent crimes.
    a. true
    b. false

4. Certain types of motives can turn a simple kidnapping into an aggravated kidnapping.
    a. true
    b. false

5. False imprisonment always requires actual use of force.
   a. true
   b. false

6. Modern interpretations of the asportation element of kidnapping require only slight movement of the victim or render it virtually meaningless.
   a. true
   b. false

7. At common law, the offense of kidnapping had only three elements.
   a. true
   b. false

8. At common law, a man could not be guilty of raping his wife.
   a. true
   b. false

9. Rape law reform began seriously in the 1920s.
   a. true
   b. false

10. In some jurisdictions, an aggravated rape is one where the rapist is armed or the victim suffers serious bodily injury.
    a. true
    b. false

11. The *actus reus* of assault is offensive touching.
    a. true
    b. false

12. False imprisonment is a vicarious liability crime.
    a. true
    b. false

13. The most famous kidnapping case of the 1970s was the kidnapping and murder of Charles Lindbergh's infant son.
    a. true
    b. false

14. One difference between false imprisonment and kidnapping is that only kidnapping requires asportation of the victim.
    a. true
    b. false

15. At common law, the crime of rape was punishable by death.
    a. true
    b. false

16. At common law, rape was a specific intent crime.
    a. true
    b. false

17. If the rape victim is mentally deficient, incapacitated by alcohol or drugs, or otherwise not capable of giving a valid consent, it can still be rape even though no force was used or threatened.
    a. true
    b. false

18. Beginning in the 1990s, most states began repealing their rape shield laws.
    a. true
    b. false

19. Over time, the reasonable resistance standard came to be replaced by an utmost resistance standard.
    a. true
    b. false

20. The Model Penal Code definition of rape eliminated lack of consent as an element.
    a. true
    b. false

21. In most modern rape laws, lack of consent of the victim is not a circumstance element.
    a. true
    b. false

22. The extrinsic force standard requires more force than the intrinsic force standard.
    a. true
    b. false

23. Only a few states allow the defense of reasonable mistake of age in statutory rape cases.
    a. true
    b. false

24 Victim consent is a defense to statutory rape.
    a. true
    b. false

25. In a statutory rape case, the prosecution must prove some force or threat of force by the defendant to convict.
    a. true
    b. false

Fill in the blank

1. The term ___________ means carrying away.

2. _____________ rape involves sex with a young person, even without force.

3. The only two common law sex offenses were rape and ________.

4. The circumstance element of most modern rape laws is ________ of the victim.

5. The *actus reus* of rape is sexual ____________ of the victim.

6. In some states, a reasonable mistake of fact with regard to the victim's ________ is a defense to statutory rape.

7. Intentionally restraining someone's liberty is the offense of ____________ imprisonment.

8. The actus reus of traditional assault is a/n ____________ or threatened battery.

9. Rape ____________ laws limit evidence about a rape victim's past and reputation.

10. The _______________ standard requires more force than just the force needed to penetrate the victim.

11. Most sex crime statutes today are ____________ neutral.

12. If mistake as to the victim's age is a defense to rape, the mistake or belief must be ____________.

13. In general, assaults or batteries that cause ____________ bodily injury are felonies.

14. ____________ threats cannot be an assault, because the threat of harm is not immediate.

15. The ____________ force standard requires only the force necessary to cause penetration of the victim.

Essay

1. Why was the English case of Regina v. Morgan controversial? Do you agree or disagree with the final holding in that case?

2. Over time, how has the law of rage changed with regard to force and consent?

3. Discuss the issue of whether rape should be a specific intent crime with regard to consent.

4. How has the law of rape and rape prosecutions changed over the years?

5. Compare and contrast the elements of rape at common law with the typical rape statute today.

CHAPTER 10 ANSWER KEY

Multiple Choice

1—c (364)	2—b (364)	3—a (368)	4—d (367)	5—c (367)
6—c (333)	7—d (333)	8—b (354)	9—b (339)	10—c (345)
11—d (349)	12—a (334)	13—b (336)	14—a (357)	15—d (337)
16—b (362)	17—a (359)	18—c (349)	19—c (359)	20—a (335)
21—b (345)	22—a (338)	23—a (353)	24—b (353)	25—b (335)
26—d (354)	27—b (355)	28—c (367)	29—c (363)	30—c (363)

True-False

1—F (359)	2—F (363)	3—T (367)	4—T (367)	5—F (368)
6—T (364)	7—F (363)	8—T(337)	9—F (336)	10—T (334)
11—F (353)	12—F (367)	13—F (363)	14—T (364)	15—T (334)
16—F (335)	17—T (337)	18—F (337)	19—F (337)	20—T (338)
21—F (339)	22—T (339)	23—T (349)	24—F (349)	25—F (349)

Fill in the blank

1—asportation (364)	2—statutory (349)	3—sodomy (334)	4—nonconsent (339)
5—penetration (339)	6—age (349)	7—false (367)	8—attempted (353)
9—shield (337)	10—extrinsic force (339)	11—gender (338)	12—reasonable (349)
13—serious (354)	14—conditional (355)	15—intrinsic (339)	

Chapter 11 Crimes Against Property

LEARNING OBJECTIVES

After studying this chapter, students will

1. understand the history of theft and related offenses.
2. know the various types of modern theft and related offenses.
3. be familiar with the offense of receiving stolen property.
4. know the elements of forgery and uttering.
5. understand the crime of robbery.
6. know the definition of the offense of extortion.
7. be able distinguish robbery and extortion.
8. know the history of the crime of burglary.
9. understand the evolution and current form of the crime of burglary.
10 know the basic idea of the offense of criminal trespass.
11. be familiar with the crimes of arson and criminal mischief.

KEY WORDS AND CONCEPTS

Larceny—wrongful taking and carrying away; p. 375
Tangible property—personal property, valuable possessions, property valuable in itself; p. 378
Intangible property—property of value only because it represents something else; p. 375
Robbery—taking property from someone by threat or force; p. 375
White-collar crimes—crimes committed by persons of high occupational status; p. 375
Trespassory taking—wrongful taking; p. 375
Asportation—carrying away; p. 375
Taking—getting control; p. 376
Carrying away—moving it; p. 376
Joyriding—taking vehicle without intent to permanently deprive owner; p. 378
Grand larceny—felony theft; p. 379
Petty larceny—misdemeanor theft; p. 379
Bailee—person who has possession but not ownership of property; p. 379
Embezzlement—form of theft by employees (esp. bank employees); p. 379
Conversion—keeping something unlawfully; p. 380
False pretenses—form of theft involving deceit of victim; p. 380
Theft by deceit—another name for false pretenses; p. 380
Theft—stealing the property of another; p. 383
Intellectual property—information, formulas, designs, etc.; p. 386
Receiving stolen property—crime of obtaining property knowing it was stolen; p. 390
Fence—person who sells stolen property; p. 390
Forgery—altering a document or creating a false document; p. 394
Uttering—passing a forged document; p. 394
Extortion—unlawfully obtaining property by threat of future harm to victim; p. 402
Arson—unlawfully burning a building; p. 403
Criminal mischief—damaging or destroying personal property; p. 403
Malicious mischief—another name for criminal mischief; p. 406

Burglary—entering building of another with intent to commit felony therein; p. 408
Criminal trespass—unwanted presence on property of another; p. 408
Breaking—violent entry; p. 410
Remaining—can be criminal trespass if ordered to leave; p. 410
Surreptitious remaining—hiding in a building till others leave; p. 410
Predicate crime—crime the burglar intended to commit once inside; p. 415
Computer trespass statutes—modern statutes aimed at protecting computers; p. 416

CHAPTER OUTLINE

I. Crimes against the property of others are of three general types: taking, damaging or destroying, and invading.

II. Crimes involving taking other people's property have a long history.
- A. History of property crimes.
    1. Simple rural, agricultural society needed protection against sneaking away with (larceny) someone else's property.
    2. As society grew more complex and more personal property and more kinds of property appeared, other ways to steal the property of others became serious problems.
        - a. Taking someone else's property by force
        - b. Caretakers (bailees) taking someone else's property that was handed over to them voluntarily
            - (1) Abuse-of-trust crimes
            - (2) White-collar crimes
- B. Larceny
    1. *Actus reus*—taking and carrying away
    2. *Mens rea*—intent to permanently deprive someone else of their property
    3. Circumstance element—property (something of value)
        - a. Tangible personal property (property valuable itself like a ring)
        - b. Intangible personal property (paper that represents something of value, like stocks, bonds, checks)
        - c. Services (like telephone service)
        - d. Labor
- C. White-collar (higher occupation-related) crimes
    1. Embezzlement (first white-collar crime)
        - a. Keeping (converting) property lawfully obtained
        - b. "Converting" substitutes for "taking" in larceny
    2. False pretenses (theft by deceit)
        - a. Tricking (deceiving) someone into giving up their property
        - b. Deceiving substitutes for taking in larceny and converting in embezzlements
- D. Theft
    1. Modern consolidated theft statutes—turn away from history to logic in consolidating embezzlement larceny, and false pretenses into one crime of theft: getting other people's money by taking, converting, or deceiving.

2. Identity theft
    a. New way of committing an old crime—take someone else's property by first stealing their identity
    b. Key to identity theft—get victims' personal information
    c. Sources for stealing personal information—family members, friends, neighbors
    d. Sources for stealing other people's property—credit cards, utility services, bank accounts.
3. Theft by computers and the Internet
    a. Computers and the Internet—created sources of great good but also great potential for evil by creating new means to get other people's property
    b. Some states' response is to expand the definition of traditional theft.
    c. Most states have created specific statutes aimed at stealing by means of computers and the Internet.

E. Receiving stolen property
1. It is a crime not only to take someone else's property but also to "receive" (accept) property already stolen.
2. *Actus reus*—receiving means controlling (not necessarily physically) property
3. *Mens rea* varies from knowingly to recklessly to negligently, depending on the state.
4. *Mens rea* also includes the intent to keep the property permanently.

F. Forgery and uttering
1. Forgery
    a. Elements
        (1) *Actus reus*—making a false document
        (2) *Mens rea*—intent to get someone else's property
    b. "Document" expanded in some statutes to anything that can be falsified.
2. Uttering
    a. Elements
        (1) *Actus reus*—passing or using a forged document
        (2) *Mens rea*—intent to defraud (get other people's property) by passing or using the forgery
    b. Utterer doesn't have to alter the document.

G. Robbery
1. Crimes against persons and property
2. Robbery elements
    a. *Actus reus*—taking and carrying away someone else's property by force or threat of immediate force
    b. *Mens rea*—intent to take property from another person by force or threat of immediate force
    c. Degrees measured by
        (1) Force (kind and degree) used
        (2) Injury (kind and degree) inflicted

H. Extortion (blackmail)
  1. Crimes against persons and their property
  2. Extortion elements
    a. *Actus reus*—taking someone else's property by threat of a variety of future harms
    b. *Mens rea*—intent to take someone else's property by threat of future harm

III. Arson, and criminal mischief are two typical crimes involving damaging and destroying other people's property.
  A. Crimes of damaging or destroying buildings (arson) and personal (tangible) property (criminal mischief)
  B. Arson elements
    1. *Actus reus*—"burning" building
    2. *Mens rea*—intent to commit the act of burning or setting fire to a building (not necessary to intend to damage or destroy the building)
    3. Degrees
      a. First degree—burning occupied buildings
      b. Second degree—burning unoccupied structures
  C. Criminal mischief
    1. Three kinds of harm to tangible property
      a. Damage or destruction by fire, explosives, or "dangerous acts"
      b. Tampering so as to endanger tangible property
      c. Deception or threat that causes monetary loss
    2. Other elements
      a. *Actus reus*—burning, exploding, or other dangerous act
      b. *Actus reus*—tampering or endangering by deceit or threat
      c. *Mens rea*—purposely, knowingly, recklessly, or negligently doing any of the acts

IV. The crimes of burglary and criminal trespass involve invading other people's property.
  A. Invasion of property is the heart of burglary and criminal trespass.
  B. Burglary and criminal trespass are crimes even if someone else's property is not taken, damaged, or destroyed.
  C. Burglary
    1. History
      a. Originated as a crime of nighttime invasion of homes (regarded as deserving special protection, especially at night).
      b. Grew to include invasions of all kinds of buildings and vessels at any time of day or night.
    2. Elements
      a. *Actus reus*—entering or remaining in (and in a few states "breaking into") someone else's "structure"
      b. *Mens rea*—intent to commit a crime once inside ("crime" intended varies widely from "felony" to "any violation of law")

3. Circumstance elements
    a. Structure includes more than homes ("any structure, any building, vessels, and vehicles").
    b. Structure has to be someone else's.
4. Degree (grading) depends on
    a. What type of dwelling
    b. Whether a weapon was used
    c. Whether the dwelling was occupied
    d. Whether the occupant was assaulted
    e. Whether a crime was intended once inside

D. Criminal trespass
1. Essence of the offense—unwanted presence
2. Elements
    a. *Actus reus*—unauthorized entering or remaining in someone else's premises (definition of premises differs from state to state)
    b. *Mens rea* varies
        (1) Knowledge of lack of authority (most states)
        (2) Specific intent to enter or remain to commit a crime without authority
        (3) Strict liability
3. Degrees (grading) depends on
    a. Whether the trespass was of a home at night—misdemeanor
    b. Whether the dwelling was an occupied structure—petty misdemeanor
    c. Whether there was a "no trespass" notice—violation
4. Computer trespass
    a. Unauthorized access by hackers to computer information systems
    b. No need to prove destruction or damage
    c. Invasion itself is the essence of the crime.

CHAPTER SUMMARY

Crimes against property are one of three types: taking it, damaging or destroying it, or invading it. Since the 1600s many new ways to steal have arisen. The new crimes created to deal with the new problems of property crime are really only new ways of committing the three original types of crimes. Computer and Internet crimes consist of taking, damaging or destroying, or invading other people's computers or the information stored on them.

All crimes of taking property descend from larceny—the ancient common law crime of sneaking away with (stealing) someone else's property. Larceny was born as the common-law instrument to protect the Anglo-Saxons' most valuable possession—livestock.

Theft (or larceny) is a specific-intent crime; it requires the intent to permanently deprive the other person of their property. Larceny *actus reus* consists of two parts: 1. taking and 2. carrying away (asportation).

Obtaining property already stolen by someone else still is regarded as a crime. Traditionally, it was called receiving stolen property. Over time a number of new property crimes emerged as taking other people's property. Embezzlement was not a common law crime; it was created by Parliament. Embezzlement involves converting another's property with intent to permanently deprive the owner of the property. Conversion means keeping someone else's property that was initially legally obtained and then illegally keeping it for one's own benefit.

The crime of false pretenses involves the intent to permanently deprive owner of property by using deceit or false representations. This, however, is not the only crime that involves attempting to cheat people by deception.

Taking other people's money by making false documents is called forgery. The uttering or passing of false or forged documents is also a crime. Forgery consists of making false legal documents or altering existing ones, such as checks, deeds, stocks, bonds, and credit cards. This is done for the purpose of getting someone else's property. Uttering means to pass false documents on to others.

Robbery is a crime against persons and their property. It involves taking someone else's property from their person by force or the threat of immediate force. Robbery consists of three elements. The *actus reus* has a number of components. They are 1. the taking and carrying away, 2. by immediate force or the threat of immediate force, 3. another person's property from their body or presence. The *mens rea* is the intent to permanently deprive the victim of their property by immediate force or the threat of immediate force. The circumstance element is that the property is taken from the victim's person or presence

Extortion (also called blackmail) is a crime against persons and their property. Theft by extortion is taking someone else's property by threats of future harm. Time separates extortion from robbery: robbery is a threat to hurt someone right now if they don't give up their property; extortion is a threat to hurt someone later. The elements of extortion consist of: 1. *Mens rea*. The specific intent to take someone else's property by means of threats; 2. *Actus reus*. A specific threat by which the taking of property is accomplished.

Arson (damaging or destroying other people's buildings by fire, explosives, is a felony. Criminal mischief (destroying or tampering with other people's property or causing money loss by "expensive practical jokes" or false threats) is a misdemeanor. Criminal mischief includes three types of harm to tangible property: 1. destruction or damage by fire, explosives, or other "dangerous acts" (the original malicious mischief), 2. tampering with tangible property so as to endanger it; and 3. deception or threat that causes monetary loss.

The elements of common-law burglary from which our modern burglary emerged included: 1. breaking and entering (*actus reus*) 2. the dwelling of another (circumstance element) 3. in the nighttime (circumstance element) 4. with the intent to commit a felony inside (*mens rea*). Modern burglary has outgrown its common-law origin of just protecting homes. Now, you can "burglarize" all kinds of structures, even vehicles, at any time of the day. The breaking and entering elements have been eliminated or modified, and the predicate crimes do not always have to be a felony.

A less serious crime related to burglary is criminal trespass. The *actus reus* of criminal trespass is the unauthorized entering of or remaining on the premises of another. The *mens rea* varies, including 1. knowingly enters or remains without authority invitation, license privilege, or legality 2. specific intent to enter or remain without authority for some unlawful purpose (a few states) or 3. strict liability.

PRACTICE TEST BANK

Multiple Choice

1. A person who receives stolen property and then resells it is called a _____.
   a. unlawful receiver
   b. unlawful wholesaler
   c. larceny receptor
   d. fence

2. At common law, the offense of burglary _____.
   a. could only be committed at night
   b. included all types of buildings
   c. required entering but not breaking
   d. was a strict liability crime

3. Under modern approaches to burglary, assuming all the other elements, if the burglar entered the building unlawfully in an unusual fashion, such as coming down the chimney, this _____.
   a. could not be a burglary because there was no breaking
   b. could be a burglary but only if the building was occupied
   c. could still be a burglar
   d. is not a burglary because there was no unlawful entry

4. In many states and the Model Penal Code, the *actus reus* of arson requires _____.
   a. only that the defendant start a fire
   b. that some part of the building be charred
   c. that some damage to the building occur
   d. that some part of the building be burned

5 At common law, the intent to commit a crime in the dwelling required that the intended crime be _____.
   a. a crime of violence
   b. a felony
   c. any form of theft
   d. any property crime

6. In contrast to earlier law burglary law, by 1900, _____.
   a. the breaking element became a mere technicality
   b. evolved into a strict liability offense
   c. eliminated the requirement of intent to commit a crime in the building
   d. required that the building be occupied at the time of the burglary

7. In addition to the unlawful entry version of burglary, the Model Penal Code and some jurisdictions also have a/n_______ version of burglary.
   a. surreptitious remaining
   b. constructive concealment
   c. constructive burglary
   d. entry by deceit

8. Parliament created the crime of ________ to deal with bank tellers and similar employees who wrongfully appropriated the money that lawfully came into their possession but really belonged to others.
   a. larceny
   b. embezzlement
   c. false pretenses
   d. extortion

9. Illegally obtaining property by deception, trick or lie is called _____.
   a. theft by trick
   b. false pretenses
   c. larceny by deception
   d. larceny by lie

10. Most states have attempted to better organize theft law by enacting _________ statutes.
    a. omnibus larceny
    b. comprehensive larceny
    c. complete theft
    d. consolidated theft

11. The specific intent element of receiving stolen property is _____.
    a. knowing the property is stolen
    b. receiving property
    c. deceiving the true owner
    d. finding property that is stolen

12. The *actus reus* of larceny has two components: _____.
    a. intent to steal and intent to deprive the owner
    b. possession and concealing
    c. taking and carrying away
    d. retrieving and concealing

13. Common law larceny required ________ in the taking.
   a. a trespass
   b. deception
   c. force
   d. deceit

14. The term asportation means _____.
   a. obtaining possession
   b. receiving
   c. obtaining ownership
   d. carrying away

15. A ________ is a person who has legal possession of the property, but the owner who still retains ownership rights.
   a. finder
   b. constructive possessor
   c. constructive owner
   d. bailee

16. A _____ is a person who has the stolen property between the thief and a purchaser.
   a. fence
   b. purveyor
   c. procurer
   d. provocateur

17. The offense of burglary has ________ *mens rea* elements.
   a. two
   b. three
   c. four
   d. five

18. Which of the following elements of common law burglary is retained in most modern statutes?
   a. the burglary occurred at night
   b. the entry must be unlawful
   c. the building must be a dwelling
   d. there must be an actual, physical breaking

19. Under modern statutes, the crime the burglar intended to commit inside the building _____.
   a. must be a crime that is *mala prohibita*
   b. has been expanded beyond the common law rule of felonies only
   c. is limited to crimes of theft
   d. must be a felony as also required at common law

20. If a person is apprehended while unlawfully on someone else's property, but there is no evidence of another crime, or intent to commit another crime, the proper charge would be _____.
    a. burglary
    b. criminal trespass
    c. attempted invasion of privacy
    d. discrepancy

21. The offense of burglary is a crime _____.
    a that has no *mens rea* elements
    b. that has a general intent component but not a specific intent element
    c. that has a specific intent, but not a general intent
    d. that has both a specific and a general intent elements

22. The specific intent of robbery is intent to _____.
    a. harm the victim
    b. permanently deprive the victim of the property
    c. commit a crime
    d. obtain title to the property

23. One of the circumstance elements of burglary is _____.
    a. type of structure
    b. constructive breaking
    c. intent to enter unlawfully
    d. surreptitious remaining

24. Which of the following are *mens rea* elements of burglary?
    a intent to damage or destroy the building
    b intent to break and enter or surreptitiously remain
    c intent to deprive the owner of possession and ownership of the structure
    d. intent to surprise and harm the persons in the structure

25. As compared to burglary, criminal trespass has _____.
    a. fewer elements
    b. greater penalties
    c. more elements
    d. a longer history

26. The *mens rea* in most types of arson is intent to _____.
    a. destroy a building by fire
    b. enter a building to start a fire
    c. set a fire to a building
    d. break into a building and start a fire

27. The defendant walks into the bank while it is open to the public and hides in the public restroom. After the bank closes he attempts break into the vault. This is the _________ type of burglary.
   a. privileged entry
   b. surreptitious remaining
   c. false pretenses
   d. constructive entry

28. Many incidents that were burglaries at common law would today _____.
   a. be criminal trespasses
   b. not be crimes
   c. be *mala in se* crimes
   d. also be burglaries

29. The law of criminal trespass has been expanded beyond its traditional coverage to now include ______ trespass.
   a. real cstatc
   b. personal property
   c. computer
   d. curtilage

30. The crime of uttering means _____.
   a. speaking false words to commit theft by deception
   b. passing a forged document
   c. forging a document
   d. stealing tangible property

True/False

1. At common law, walking through a wide open door into a home to commit a felony therein was a burglary.
   a. true
   b. false

2. To be guilty of burglary, the burglar does not have to complete the crime he intended to commit.
   a. true
   b. false

3. The modern definition of burglary is narrower than the common law definition.
   a. true
   b. false

4. The two offenses that involve both thefts and force or threat of force are robbery and burglary.
   a. true
   b. false

5. Picking a pocket without any additional action or force by the defendant is not a robbery.
   a. true
   b. false

6. In some states, a purse snatching where the victim is not threatened and does not resist and the purse is not otherwise attached to the person, is not a robbery.
   a. true
   b. false

7. The crime of uttering involves passing forged documents.
   a. true
   b. false

8. Robbery requires that the robber threaten to use force immediately.
   a. true
   b. false

9. The *mens rea* of extortion is the specific intent to obtain property by deceit.
   a. true
   b. false

10. The definition of arson has contracted as compared to its definition at common law.
    a. true
    b. false

11. Most arson statutes create specific, intent crimes.
    a. true
    b. false

12. The *actus reus* of arson is to set fire to a structure.
    a. true
    b. false

13. Extortion is a strict liability crime.
    a. true
    b. false

14. Many states divide arson into one or more degrees or types.
    a. true
    b. false

15. Surreptitious remaining is a type of extortion.
    a. true
    b. false

16. Embezzlement was a crime at common law.
    a. true
    b. false

17. For common law burglary, a *mens rea* element was that the crime occurred at night.
    a. true
    b. false

18. Until the 1900s, the *actus reus* of burglary consisted of only constructive breaking.
    a. true
    b. false

19. At common law, the breaking element of burglary was by a surreptitious remaining element.
    a. true
    b. false

20. Robbery is a crime against both persons and property.
    a. true
    b. false

21. Robbery has a specific intent element.
    a. true
    b. false

22. Robbery has a circumstance element.
    a. true
    b. false

23. While picking a pocket, the thief is grabbed by the victim. The thief pushes the victim away and takes the wallet. This is a robbery.
    a. true
    b. false

24. Most robbery victims are physically harmed.
    a. true
    b. false

25. The *actus reus* of uttering is transferring or passing a forged document.
    a. true
    b. false

Fill in the blank

1. The common law *mens rea* of arson was that it be done willfully and ____________.

2. Some states have removed the unlawful ___________ element to create a new form of burglary by surreptitious remaining.

3. The Model Penal Code limits the crime of burglary to _______ structures or vehicles.

4 The ___________ crime is the crime the burglar intends to commit inside the building.

5. The illegal use or keeping of someone else's property is called _______.

6. The form of theft involving lies or deception is called ______________________.

7. Robbery involves taking property from the person of the victim or ___________.

8. The term ___________ means to pass or transfer a writing.

9. The *actus reus* of common law burglary is breaking and ___________.

10. Many states have combined a number of types of theft into one statute that is termed a. _____________ theft statute.

11. In embezzlement, the conversion replaces the usual ___________ requirement.

12. A ___________ is a temporary possessor of personal property who doesn't own the property.

13. If a pickpocket must push or shove the victim to get the wallet the crime becomes one of ___________.

14. The crime of __________ involves unlawfully making, signing or altering documents.

15. Information, programs, and data are known as ______________ property.

Essay

1. Compare and contrast forgery, theft by deception and uttering.

2. Trace the development of the law of theft and related offenses from common law to modern codes.

3. Trace the development of the law of burglary from common law to modern codes.

4. Compare and contrast robbery and extortion.

5. Compare and contrast arson, burglary and criminal trespass.

CHAPTER 11 ANSWER KEY

Multiple Choice

1—d (390)	2—a (409)	3—c (410)	4—a (404)	5—b (409)
6—(a) 410	7—a (410)	8—b (380)	9—b (380)	10—d (383)
11—a (391)	12—c (376)	13—a (375)	14—d (375)	15—d (379)
16—a (390)	17—a (409)	18—b (410)	19—b (414)	20—b (415)
21—d (409)	22—b (398)	23—a (409)	24—b (409)	25—a (416)
26—c (403)	27—b (410)	28—d (409)	29—c (416)	30—b (397)

True-False

1—F (410)	2—T (414)	3—F (410)	4—F (409)	5—T (398)
6—T (400)	7—T (394)	8—T (398)	9—F (402)	10—F (403)
11—F (403)	12—T (403)	13—F (402)	14—T (405)	15—F (410)
16—F (379)	17—F (409)	18—F (410)	19—F (410)	20—T (398)
21—T (398)	22—T (398)	23—T (398)	24—F (398)	25—T (398)

Fill in the blank

1—maliciously (403)	2—entry (410)	3—occupied (411)	4—predicate (415)
5—conversion (380)	6—false pretenses (380)	7—presence (398)	8—utter (394)
9—entering (408)	10—consolidated (383)	11—taking (379)	12—bailee (379)
13—robbery (398)	14—forgery (395)	15—intellectual (386)	

Chapter 12 Crimes Against Public Order and Morals

LEARNING OBJECTIVES

After studying this chapter, students will

1. understand the history of public order and quality of life crimes.
2. know the difference between riot and rout.
3. be familiar with the Model Penal Code definition of disorderly conduct.
4. be familiar with the crimes of loitering and vagrancy.
5 understand the broken windows theory.
6. understand the void for vagueness doctrine.
7. be familiar with First Amendment issues in quality of life crimes.
8. understand First Amendment forum theory and the types of forums.
9. know the basic law and procedure for abating public nuisances.
10. understand the debate over the proper relationship between law and morality.
11. be familiar with the concept of victimless crimes.
12. understand prostitution and related crimes.

KEY TERMS AND CONCEPTS

Victimless crimes—adult consensual crimes, or crimes without a victim or people who feel victimized; p. 425
Individual disorderly conduct—individual public disturbance or peace crime; p. 426
Group disorderly conduct—group activity which causes public disturbance; p. 426
Breach of the peace—conduct which disturbs public peace; p. 426
Actual disorderly conduct—fighting in public, unreasonable noise; p. 426
Constructive disorderly conduct—conduct tending to provoke others to break the peace; p. 426
Unlawful assembly—unlawful gathering of 3 or more people to commit an unlawful act; p. 428
Rout—3 or more people moving together toward an unlawful act; p. 428
Riot—3 or more people committing a violent, unlawful act; p. 428
Order—acting according to ordinary standards of good manners; p. 430
Liberty—right of individuals to come and go as they please without government interference; p. 430
"Bad manners" crimes—quality of life crimes or crimes against public order; p. 430
Crimes against public order—quality of life crimes; p. 430
Quality-of-life crimes—crimes against public order or bad manners crimes; p. 430
Broken-windows theory—theory that tolerance of minor disorder leads to greater disorder; p. 30
Vagrancy—roaming about without visible means of support; p. 431
Loitering—standing around with no apparent purpose; p. 431
Preliminary injunction—temporary court order to do or stop doing something; p. 433
Panhandling—begging in public; p. 438
Content neutral, reasonable time, place, and manner regulations—permitted by First Amendment; p. 439
Expressive conduct—conduct that conveys a message; p. 439

Forums (fora)—different types of public places that trigger different levels of First Amendment protection; p. 439
Commercial speech—gets less protection than many other types of speech; p. 439
Injunction to abate public nuisances—civil remedy to deal with public nuisances and dangers, such as gang activity; p. 445
Crimes against public morals—vice crimes, includes prostitution and consensual sex crimes; p. 455
Wolfendon Report—English report recommending decriminalization of consensual sex crimes between adults; p. 455
Prostitution—buying or selling sexual contact with another; p. 456
Patrons—those who buy sex ("Johns"); p. 456
Prostitutes—those who sell their sexual services; p. 456
Solicit prostitution—getting customers for or facilitating prostitution; p. 456
Promoting prostitution—pimping or pandering; p. 456

CHAPTER OUTLINE

I. Issues of public order include three major types of crimes.
- A. Disorderly conduct crimes
- B. Quality-of-life crimes
- C. Victimless crimes

II. Disorderly conduct crimes can involved group or individual activity.
- A. Historically, these were largely ignored misdemeanors.
- B. Purposes for Model Penal Code provision
    - 1. Define *actus reus* more precisely than "disorderly conduct"
    - 2. Add a *mens rea* element to what used to be strict liability offenses
- C. Individual disorderly conduct in Model Penal Code
    - 1. *Actus reus*—three kinds
        - a. Fighting
        - b. Making unreasonable noise, using offensive language
        - c. Creating hazardous or offensive conditions
    - 2. *Mens rea*—acting purposely, knowingly, or recklessly
    - 3. Special individual disorderly conduct sections in Model Penal Code
        - a. Knowingly spreading false alarms
        - b. Appearing drunk in public (no *mens rea* requirement)
        - c. Loitering or prowling (no *mens rea* requirement)
        - d. Purposely or recklessly obstructing highways or other public passages
    - e. Purposely disrupting lawful meetings, processions, or gatherings
- D. Group disorderly conduct ("riot")
    - 1. Background
        - a. Three ancient misdemeanor crimes (unlawful assembly, rout, riot)
        - b. Riot Act of 1714—made riot a felony
        - c. "Reading the riot act" comes from this act

2. Elements
    a. *Actus reus*—participate in disorderly conduct
    b. *Mens rea*
        (1) Have specific intent or purpose to commit or facilitate the commission of a felony
        (2) Have the purpose to prevent or coerce an official action
        (3) Have knowledge that any participant used or plans to use a deadly weapon

III. "Quality of life" crimes involved both constitutional and criminological concerns.
A. These crimes attempt to control "bad manners" in public places (sidewalks, streets, parks).
B. Ancient offenses (crimes against public order) applied to new situations ("street people" and "gangs") called by a new name ("quality-of-life crimes").
C. They underscore the tension between liberty and order in a constitutional democracy.
D. Are the application of due process of liberty (Chapter 2) to maintaining order in public
E. "Broken windows" theory
1. Theory—There's a link between "minor" quality-of-life offenses (public drunkenness, panhandling, graffiti, vandalism, prostitution, loitering) and serious crimes (rape, robbery, burglary).
2. Reality
    a. National debate concentrates on serious crime; local officials and public more worried about quality-of-life offenses.
    b. Empirical findings mixed as to link between serious crime and disorder.
        (1) Some find a causal relationship (Kelling, Skogan).
        (2) Others find common origins but not a causal link (Sampson and Radenbush).
F. Wide public agreement on what "bad public manners" consists of
G. Vagrancy and loitering
1. Two ancient offenses aimed at roaming around (vagrancy) with no visible means of support and at standing around (loitering).
2. Vagrancy and loitering have been tailored to meet modern problems of "bad public manners" of street people and gangs.
3. Due process (void-for-vagueness) restricts power to criminalize vagrancy (Papachristou v. City of Jacksonville 1972) and loitering (Kolender v. Lawson 1983)
4. Vagrancy and loitering can overcome the vagueness objection if they're defined to include more than just roaming around or standing around.
H. Panhandling
1. Panhandling statutes call the ancient crime of public begging into service to control "aggressive" begging by "street people."
2. Bans on panhandling don't apply to "organized charities" (Salvation Army)
3. Panhandling is "speech" protected by the First Amendment.
    a. Right to panhandle is "commercial speech," and so it's less protected than other types of speech.

b. States can control time, place (subways), and manner ("aggressive") of panhandling.
c. States have limited ability control the content of panhandling (the right to ask for money).

I. Street gangs
1. "Bands of loitering youth" scare ordinary people
2. Anti-gang ordinances raise due process questions (liberty and void for vagueness).
3. Anti-gang ordinances meet due process and liberty requirements if they define loitering more specifically than "hanging out with no apparent purpose" (permissible to ban loitering "for the purpose of committing a crime").

IV. "Victimless" crimes are a controversial topic.
A. Applies only to adults
B. Refers to crimes committed by adults who don't see themselves as victims
C. Referring to these crimes as "victimless" is controversial and involves the debate over the proper relationship between law and morality.
D. The Wolfendon Report in 1950s England recommended decriminalizing private sexual conduct between consenting adults (to homosexuality and prostitution).
E. Today, both patrons and prostitutes (male or female) commit prostitution, but it is a crime almost everywhere in the U.S.

CHAPTER SUMMARY

Today's disorderly conduct crimes have the same names as and similar meanings as their ancient English ancestors: the misdemeanor of individual disorderly conduct and the felony of group disorderly conduct (riot).

The Model Penal Code was very influential in shaping the current law. The code limits conduct that qualifies as disorderly conduct *actus reus* to three kinds: 1. fighting in public, 2. making unreasonable noise or using abusive language, 3. creating a "hazardous or physically offensive condition" like strewing garbage, setting off "stink bombs," or turning off lights in crowded public places. The code was also unusual in that it had a *mens rea* element.

In practice, the most common use of disorderly conduct laws is against fighting in public. Fighting can cause two harms: disturbing community peace and disturbing or endangering innocent bystanders.

Group disorderly conduct consisted of three misdemeanors at the common law: unlawful assembly, rout, and riot. All three were aimed at preventing the ultimate evil of open disorder and breach of the public peace. Unlawful assembly was committed when a group of at least three persons joined together for the purpose of committing an unlawful act. If the group of three or more started toward achieving their purpose, they committed the crime of rout. If the group actually committed an unlawful violent act, or performed a lawful act in a "violent or tumultuous manner," they committed the crime of riot (if there were twelve of them). Committing riot didn't require the group to plan their unlawful violent act in advance. It was enough that once together they came up with the plan of violence.

Some disorderly conduct crimes are now called "quality of life" crimes, but they're still aimed at the same conduct—"bad manners" in public places. Efforts to control bad manners in public underscore the tension between order and liberty in constitutional democracies. Order is acting in accordance with ordinary standards of good manners and decency. Liberty is freedom to come and go and do as we like without government interference. The U.S. Supreme Court has used the term "ordered liberty" to describe this need for both.

Quality-of-life crimes are minor offenses, but the "broken windows" theory claims (based on mixed empirical results) they're linked to serious crime. In the 1980s, two scholars noted a deep public need for what they called a lost sense of public "good manners," especially in our largest cities. Professors James Q. Wilson and George L. Kelling (1982) suggested that what were labeled "petty crimes" weren't just "bothering" law-abiding people; they were connected to serious crime. They called this connection between disorderly conduct and serious crime the broken-windows theory. According to Kelling, research conducted since the article was written in 1982 has demonstrated a direct link between public disorder and crime. Others argue that both disorder and serious crime are caused by the same factors and that disorder does not always lead to serious crime.

There is widespread public support among all classes, races, and communities for controlling the offensive behaviors of "street people" and "street gangs." Most people are more worried about bad public manners (loitering, panhandling, public drunkenness, and prostitution) than they are about serious crimes (rape, robbery, burglary, and assault).

A number of state and city governments have passed criminal laws to regulate gang behavior. In some places, it's a crime to participate in a gang. Some statutes and ordinances have stiffened the penalties for crimes committed by gang members. Others make it a crime to encourage minors to participate in gangs. Some have applied organized crime statutes to gangs. A few have punished parents for their children's gang activities. Cities have also passed ordinances banning gang members from certain public places, particularly city parks.

Laws against loitering, vagrancy, panhandling and non-criminal gang activity raise serious issues of due process (void-for-vagueness) and violation of First Amendment rights. Many loitering, vagrancy, panhandling and anti-gang laws have been found to be unconstitutional. However, carefully written laws that are specific and are content-neutral time, place, and manner restrictions can be constitutional if other outlets for expression are available.

Government ability to regulate speech, including panhandling, varies with the type of public property involved. In traditional public forums, government power is weakest. Traditional public forums include public parks and streets. Government power is at an intermediate level in designate public forums. These are public places that the government has set aside or designated for speech activities. Auditoriums or public bulletin boards would be examples. Government power is strongest in nonpublic forums such as government office buildings and military bases.

In addition to criminal penalties, cities have also turned to civil remedies to control gang activity. For example, in the ancient civil remedy injunction to abate public nuisances, which is still used, government attorneys ask courts to declare gang activities and gang members public nuisances and to issue injunctions (court orders) to abate (stop) the public nuisance.

There is inherent conflict between the societal values of freedom or liberty on the one hand and order and security on the other. Both cannot be maximized at the same time. The problem is trying to strike a balance between the two. The U.S. Supreme Court uses the term "ordered liberty" to reflect the need for accommodation of both. This is also reflected in the debate between Stephen and Mill over the proper relationship of law to morality. Those who favor individual liberty (such as Mill) disapprove of using law to enforce morality. Those who feel that morality is important for keeping society together (Stephen) approve of using law to enforce morality.

"Victimless" crimes (the ancient "crimes against public morals") are a controversial issue. It pits those who believe the criminal law should enforce morality against those who believe the private, nonviolent, consensual behavior of competent adults is none of the law's business. The Wolfendon Report, a British report from the 1950s, recommended that private consensual adult homosexuality and prostitution be decriminalized.

Victimless crimes include crimes between consenting adults, and/or crimes in which the victim does not perceive of themselves as being a victim. A number of types of offenses have been termed victimless. Among these are substance abuse, Internet censorship, loitering, prostitution, sodomy, seat belt law violations, helmet law violations, bans on bungee jumping, and laws against assisted suicide. Crimes involving a willing buyer and seller, such as prostitution, drug and firearms crimes can also be victimless crimes.

Prostitution is an ancient business, prospering in all cultures at all times in spite of being illegal. It's also a crime nearly everywhere in the United States. Prostitution used to be reserved for the act of selling sexual intercourse for money—and only selling, not buying, sex was included. Now it means all contacts and penetrations as long as they're done with the intent to gratify sexual appetite. Both patrons (buyers) and prostitutes (sellers) can commit prostitution. In the past, the law recognized only women as prostitutes. Now both men and women who sell sex are prostitutes.

It's a crime not only to buy and sell sex, but also to solicit prostitution (sometimes called promoting prostitution, or "pimping," or "pandering"). Soliciting prostitution means getting customers for prostitutes and/or providing a place for prostitutes and customers to engage in sex for money. Prostitution and promoting prostitution are misdemeanors in most states, but it's a serious felony when circumstances like minors and violence are involved.

PRACTICE TEST BANK

Multiple Choice

1. The ________ theory suggests that public order crime should be policed aggressively because it eventually triggers increases in more serious crimes, and thus stopping public order crimes is important in protecting the quality of life in a community.
   a. shattered dreams
   b. unmended fences
   c. broken windows
   d. cracked sidewalks

2. Crimes against morals and public order termed _______ crimes.
   a. public disturbance
   b. breach of the peace
   c. public life
   d. quality of life

3. Broken windows theory was formulated by _____.
   a. Boyce and Hart
   b. Wilson and Kelling
   c. LaFave and Scott
   d. Fulbright and Jaworski

4. Starting in the 1960s, courts began striking down vagrancy laws because they violated the ________ doctrine.
   a. cruel and unusual punishment
   b. void for vagueness
   c. *ex post facto* law
   d. *res ipsa loquitur*

5. One of the First Amendment requirements for a valid time, place and manner regulation is that the regulation _____.
   a . be content neutral
   b. serve any type of government interest
   c. be limited to places that are nonpublic forums
   d. apply only to symbolic speech

6. The term "panhandling" means _____.
   a. threatening others
   b. aggressive marketing
   c. begging
   d. stealing housewares

7. Because begging is clearly speech, attempts to regulate it must meet the requirements of the ________ Amendment.
   a. First
   b. Fourth
   c. Fifth
   d. Eighth

8. In attempting to deal with gang problems, many cities have utilized the civil remedy of an injunction to abate _____.
   a. public order crimes
   b. public nuisances
   c. quality of life crimes
   d. breaches of the peace

9. In contrast to the broken windows theory, Skogan suggests that disorder (public order crime) _____.
   a. and more serious crime are not related in any way
   b. and more serious crime may both be caused by some other factor
   c. is caused by serious crime
   d. causes more serious crime

10. One of the reasons the 7th Circuit Court of Appeals upheld the anti-panhandling ordinance in Gresham v. Peterson was because the ordinance _____.
   a. met the standards of the rational basis test
   b. banned panhandling totally at all times and places
   c. banned only panhandling where the other person was touched by the panhandler
   d. did not ban panhandling at all times and places

11. In Morales v. Chicago, the U.S. Supreme Court held that the city's anti-gang ordinance was unconstitutional because it _____.
   a. violated equal protection in that it discriminated against gang members
   b. discriminated against young people in violation of equal protection
   c. was unconstitutionally vague
   d. was an unreasonable interference with First Amendment rights

12. The expression 'reading the riot act' comes from the British Riot Act of _____.
   a. 1615
   b. 1714
   c. 1813
   d. 1912

13. The crime of vagrancy refers to _____.
   a. persons standing around with no obvious purpose
   b. being poor and being seen in public
   c. being homeless
   d. poor people roaming around with no visible means of support

14. The crime of loitering refers to _____.
   a. being without any visible means of support or employment
   b. being homeless
   c. remaining in one place with no apparent purpose
   d. panhandling

15. Traditional vagrancy and loitering statutes were struck down by the U.S. Supreme Court because such statutes violated the _____.
   a. void-for-vagueness doctrine
   b. First Amendment
   c. right of interstate travel
   d. Eighth Amendment

16. Under the First Amendment, panhandling is deemed to be _____ speech which gets only a low level of protection.
   a. symbolic
   b. political
   c. expressive
   d. commercial

17. A civil approach to attacking the gang problem involves an _____ to abate public nuisances.
   a. interlocutory decree
   b. injunction
   c. invective
   d. infraction

18. The term victimless crime typically only applies to behavior by _____.
   a. the poor
   b. minors
   c. adults
   d. gang members

19. In Britain in the 1950s, the _____ Report recommended decriminalizing prostitution and consensual homosexual behavior.
   a. Whittendon
   b. Whittington
   c. Wolverton
   d. Wolfendon

20. Most modern prostitution laws _____.
   a. cover both the buyer and seller
   b. are limited to selling sexual penetrations
   c. are felonies for the first offense
   d. apply only when a minor is involved

21. Today's disorderly conduct statutes grew out of the common law crime of _____.
    a. disturbing the public peace
    b. breach of the peace
    c. public indecency
    d. public disorder

22. The Model Penal Code approach to disorderly conduct differs from prior approaches in that the code includes _____.
    a. an *actus reus* element
    b. felony punishment
    c. a *mens rea* element
    d. starting a riot

23. At common law, the offense of unlawful assembly involved ____ or more persons joined together for the purpose of committing an unlawful act.
    a. two
    b. three
    c. four
    d. five

24. At common law, if the people committing an unlawful assembly starting moving toward achieving an illegal purpose the offense became a _____.
    a. riot
    b. rout
    c. unlawful gathering
    d. unlawful congregation

25. Under the British Riot Act of 1714, the felony offense of riot required participation of _____or more persons.
    a. three
    b. six
    c. nine
    d. twelve

26. Government power to regulate speech and soliciting is weakest in public streets and parks which are known as _____.
    a. nonpublic forums
    b. forums by designation
    c. traditional public forums.
    d. free speech zones

27. The debate between Stephen and Mill concerns the propriety of using the law to _____.
    a. enforce morality
    b. change society
    c. end discrimination against the poor
    d. protect children

28. In any society, there is a tension between _____.
   a. liberty and freedom
   b. order and stability
   c. license and promiscuity
   d. liberty and order

29. A pimp would be guilty of the crime of _____.
   a. pimpery
   b. promoting prostitution
   c. public indecency
   d. public obscenity

30. Conduct that conveys a message is called symbolic speech or _____.
   a. expressive conduct
   b. expressive symbolism
   c. communicative behavior
   d. symbolic behavior

<u>True/False</u>

1. Public order and decency crimes are relatively new offenses.
   a. true
   b. false

2. Order and liberty are values that can be in conflict.
   a. true
   b. false

3. The broken windows theory was originally formulated by Stephen and Mill.
   a. true
   b. false

4. Many vagrancy and loitering laws were struck down under the due process theory of void for vagueness.
   a. true
   b. false

5. Loitering means to remain in one place with no apparent purpose.
   a. true
   b. false

6. At one time, all states had laws against vagrancy and loitering.
   a. true
   b. false

7. One of the reasons why enforcing laws against quality of life crimes is controversial is because it seems to target the poorest and weakest members of the community.
   a. true
   b. false

8. The Model Penal Code does not contain any disorderly conduct or breach of the peace crimes.
   a. true
   b. false

9. Quality of life crimes were enacted primarily in cities rather than in the country.
   a. true
   b. false

10. The Wolfendon report recommended that prostitution not be decriminalized.
   a. true
   b. true

11. Crimes against public order and morals are sometimes referred to as quality of life crimes.
   a. true
   b. false

12. The term panhandling means begging.
   a. true
   b. false

13. Among the various types of forums, First Amendment rights are strongest in nonpublc forums.
   a. true
   b. false

14. Expressive conduct is not protected by the First Amendment.
   a. true
   b. false

15. Commercial speech is not protected by the First Amendment.
   a. true
   b. false

16. To be constitutional, time, place and manner regulations must apply everywhere in the city or state.
   a. true
   b. false

17. To be constitutional, time, place and manner regulations must not be based on the content of the speech.
    a. true
    b. false

18. A preliminary injunction is a temporary court order designed to freeze the status quo pending a full trial.
    a. true
    b. false

19. As compared to traditional disorderly conduct statutes, the Model Penal Code provision on disorderly conduct is unusual in that it has a *mens rea* element.
    a. true
    b. false

20. Under old English law, an unlawful assembly consisted of at least three people.
    a. true
    b. false

21. Under old English law, those who participated in an unlawful assembly could later be guilty of the offense of rout if they started toward achieving their unlawful goal.
    a. true
    b. false

22. Under the English Riot Act of 1714, it took at least ten people to form a riot.
    a. true
    b. false

23. The U.S. Supreme Court has never struck down a vagrancy or loitering law.
    a. true
    b. false

24. San Francisco was a city that enforced quality of life crimes against street people.
    a. true
    b. false

25. Victimless crimes always involve minors.
    a. true
    b. false

Fill in the blank

1. First Amendment rights are strongest in ________________ forums.

2. As compared to other forums, First Amendment rights are weakest in ___________ forums.

3. Of the three types of forums, First Amendment rights have intermediate strength in ________________ forums.

4. Panhandling is _______ speech.

5. To be valid under the First Amendment, time place and manner restrictions must serve ___________ government interests.

6. The ________________ theory suggests that tolerance of minor offenses can lead to more serious crimes.

7. Places the government chooses to make available to the public for expressive activity are called ____________________ forums.

8. A/n __________ is a court order to do or stop doing something.

9. ___________ is remaining in one place with no apparent purpose.

10. Streets, sidewalks, and public parks are termed _________________ forums.

11 The U.S. Supreme Court's term, ordered __________, reflects the need to balance the values of freedom and order.

12. Public _______ law provides a civil remedy for many quality of life problems.

13. In Chicago v. Morales, the U.S. Supreme Court invalidated a loitering ordinance aimed at _____________________.

14. Loitering and vagrancy laws were frequently found unconstitutional under the ________ ___________________________ doctrine.

15. Nonverbal expression is also called ___________ conduct.

Essay

1. Explain the broken windows theory and provide examples.

2. What did the U.S. Supreme Court decide in City of Chicago v. Morales (1999)?

3. What is the void-for-vagueness doctrine and what impact did it have on traditional loitering and vagrancy laws?

4. Compare and contrast the three types of First Amendment forums.

5. Discuss the main points of both sides in the debate between Stephen and Mill on the relationship between law and morality.

CHAPTER 12 ANSWER KEY

Multiple Choice

1—c (430) 2—d (430) 3—b (430) 4—b (431) 5—a (439)

6—c (438) 7—a (438) 8—b (445) 9—b (430) 10—d (442)

11—c (451) 12—b (428) 13—d (431) 14—c (432) 15—a (432)

16—d (439) 17—b (445) 18—c (454) 19—d (455) 20—a (456)

21—b (426) 22—c (427) 23—b (428) 24—b (428) 25—d (428)

26—c (439) 27—a (355) 28—d (430) 29—b (456) 30—d (439)

True-False

1—T (426) 2—T (430) 3—F (430) 4—T (431) 5—T (431)

6—T (431) 7—T (432) 8—F (427) 9—T (453) 10—F (455)

11—T (429) 12—T (438) 13—F (439) 14—F (439) 15—F (439)

16—F (439) 17—T (439) 18—T (433) 19—T (427) 20—T (428)

21—T (428) 22—F (428) 23—F (432) 24—T (433) 25—F (425)

Fill in the blank

1—traditional public (439) 2—nonpublic (439) 3—designated public(439) 4—commercial (438)

5—significant (438) 6—broken windows (430) 7—designated public (439) 8—injunction (433)

9—loitering (431) 10—traditional public (439) 11—liberty (430) 12—injunction (433)

13—street gangs (447) 14—void-for-vagueness (432) 15—expressive (439)

Chapter 13 Crimes Against the State

LEARNING OBJECTIVES

After studying this chapter, students will

1. be familiar with Art. III, Sec. 3 on treason.
2. understand the historical background of the crime of treason.
3. be familiar with the elements of sedition.
4. understand the crime of sabotage.
5. understand the offense of espionage.
6. be familiar with the history and major provisions of the U.S.A. Patriot Act.
7. be familiar with the history and major provisions of the AEDPA.
8. understand some of the constitutional issues involved in recent legislation.

KEY TERMS AND CONCEPTS

USA Patriot Act—federal law aimed at fighting and preventing international terrorism; p. 463
Treason—making war on aiding those who make war on the country; p. 463
Adherence to the enemy—federal statutory version of treason; p. 465
Giving aid and comfort to the enemy—federal statutory version of treason; p. 465
Sedition—advocating the violent overthrow of government; p. 468
Seditious speech—orally urging others to violently overthrow the government; p. 468
Seditious libel—urging others to violently overthrow the government in writings; p. 468
Seditious conspiracy—agreeing with others to violently overthrow the government; p. 468
Smith Act of 1940—federal statute prohibiting conspiracy to teach seditious ideas; p. 468
Sabotage—damaging or destroying government property to hinder preparation for war; p. 479
Espionage—spying or gathering intelligence for the enemy; p. 480
Intelligence gathering—spying, another word for espionage; p. 480
Anti-Terrorism and Effective Death Penalty Act (AEDPA)—federal anti-terrorist legislation passed in 1996 in response to Oklahoma City bombing; p. 481
International terrorism—terrorist acts committed outside the U.S.; p. 482
Domestic terrorism—terrorist acts committed inside the U.S.; p. 482
Weapon of mass destruction—weapons capable of killing masses of persons; p. 482
Destructive device—bombs, grenades, rockets, missiles, mines, etc, another term for weapon of mass destruction; p. 482
Harboring or concealing terrorists—federal hide terrorists from authorities; 483
Providing material support to terrorists—federal crime to aid terrorists; p. 484

CHAPTER OUTLINE

I. There are a number of crimes against the state, both ancient and new.
  - A. The USA Patriot Act and conflicting values in our constitutional democracy
    - 1. Need for public safety and security
    - 2. Desire for privacy and freedom
  - B. Issue: how to apply enduring principles of criminal and constitutional law when terrorists and terrorist groups have killed and are still trying to kill Americans at home and abroad.
  - C. Allegiance and loyalty are especially critical during national emergencies.
  - D. The Constitution was written during times of emergency.

II. Treason is an ancient crime and is defined in the Constitution.
  - A. The only crime defined in the Constitution
  - B. After the Revolution, the new government was fragile because it was so new and needed time for loyalty and allegiance to take hold.
    - 1. England, Spain, France, and Native American nations threatened from all sides.
    - 2. Traitors, spies, and other disloyal individuals and groups threatened from within.
  - C. Authors of the Constitution had mixed feelings about treason.
    - 1. They were tough on traitors who broke allegiance and were disloyal.
    - 2. Their own ancestors had fled from religious persecution and prosecution for treason.
    - 3. Treason was broadly defined in England to include thoughts and feelings that led to prosecution of innocent people.
    - 4 Two concerns:
      - a. Repression of peaceful opposition to government
      - b. Conviction of the innocent because of perjury, passion, and/or insufficient evidence
  - D. Treason is defined in the body of Constitution, where it's very difficult to change.
  - E. Elements of treason
    - 1. *Actus reus*
      - a. Levying war against the U.S.
      - b. Giving aid and comfort to enemies of the U.S.
    - 2. *Mens rea*
      - a. Intent to give aid and comfort
      - b. For the very purpose of betraying the U.S. by means of the aid and comfort
    - 3. Proof
      - a. Two witnesses to *actus reus*
      - b. Confession in open court

III. Sedition, sabotage and espionage are additional crimes against the state.
    A. Sedition
        1. Ancient crime of "stirring up" treason (advocate violent overthrow of government) by:
            a. Speeches
            b. Writing (libel)
            c. Conspiracy
        2. In the U.S. Code, sedition includes only advocating the violent overthrow of the government.
    B. Sabotage
        1. Damaging and/or destroying property related to war and defense material, buildings, and utilities (which includes transportation and harbors)
        2. Producing defective property related to war and defense
        3. Elements
            a. *Actus reus*
                (1) Destroy
                (2) Damage
                (3) Obstruct
                (4) Interfere
                (5) Contaminate
                (6) Produce defective war or national defense materials
            b. *Mens rea*
                (1) Purposely obstruct (or any other acts in actus reus)
                (2) Knowingly obstruct (or any other acts in actus reus)
                (3) Negligently obstruct (or any other acts in actus reus)
            c. Circumstance
                (1) At war
                (2) During national emergency
    C. Espionage (spying)
        1. Definition of espionage—secret intelligence gathering by spies about foreign people, activities, and enterprises for political and military uses.
        2. U.S. Code espionage elements (at any time)
            a. *Actus reus*
                (1) Communicate
                (2) Deliver
                (3) Transmit
                (4) Attempt to communicate, deliver, or transmit intelligence (information harmful to the U.S.)
            b. *Mens rea*
                (1) Purposely injure
                (2) Reason to believe use of intelligence will injure
            c. Circumstances
                (1) Intelligence provided to foreign government
                (2) Foreign faction or party
                (3) Foreign military or naval force

        (4) Foreign representative, officer, agent, employee, subject, or citizen
    3. U.S. Code espionage elements (during war)
        a. *Actus reus*
            (1) Collect any intelligence useful to the enemy
            (2) Publish it
            (3) Communicate it
            (4) Attempt to do so
        b. *Mens rea*—intent to communicate information to enemy
        c. Circumstance—time of war

IV. A number of relatively new statutes involve fighting terrorism.
- A. General crimes applicable to terrorist acts
    - 1. Treason, sedition, sabotage, and espionage
    - 2. Murder, attempted murder, and conspiracy to murder also apply
- B. Use of weapons of mass destruction
    - 1. Elements
        - a. *Actus reus*
            - (1) Use
            - (2) Threaten to use
            - (3) Attempt or conspire to use
        - b. *Mens rea*—without lawful authority (voluntarily)
        - c. Circumstance(s)
            - (1) Against a U.S. "national" outside the U.S.
            - (2) Against any "person" inside the U.S.
            - (3) Against any property inside or outside the U.S.
    - 2. Definition of "weapon of mass destruction"
        - a. "Any destructive device"—explosive, incendiary, poison gas, bomb, grenade, rocket, missile, mine, or similar device
        - b. Any weapon intended to cause death or serious bodily injury by poisonous chemicals or precursors
        - c. Any weapon involving a disease mechanism
        - d. Any weapon designed to release radiation or radioactivity at levels harmful to human life
- C. Acts of terrorism transcending national boundaries
    - 1. Definition—conduct occurring partly inside and partly outside the U.S.
    - 2. Types of conduct (*actus reus*)
        - a. Commit violent crimes against any person inside the U.S.
        - b. Create a substantial risk of serious bodily injury by destroying or damaging property within the U.S.
        - c. Threatening, or attempting, or conspiring to commit (a) or (b)
    - 3. Circumstances
        - a. Victims—U.S. government; members of uniformed services; officials, employees, and agents of the U.S.
        - b. Property owned or leased by the U.S.

4. Penalties
    a. Death for killing or death resulting from the act
    b. Up to life for kidnapping
    c. Up to 35 years for maiming
    d. Up to 30 years for assault
    e. Up to 25 years for damaging or destroying property

D. Harboring or concealing terrorists
1. *Actus reus*—harboring or concealing persons who have committed or are about to commit a list of terrorist-related crimes
2. *Mens rea*—knowing (or a reasonable person should have known) the crimes in (1) were going to be committed
3. Penalty—fine and up to 10 years imprisonment

E. Providing material support to terrorists (§ 2339A) and terrorist organizations (§ 2339B)
1. Prosecutions for violating Section 2339B most frequent in practice
2. Material support crimes created after Oklahoma City bombing in the Anti-Terrorism and Effective Death Penalty Act (AEDPA) of 1996
3. Amendment increased the AEDPA penalty in the USA Patriot Act (Uniting and Strengthening America by Providing Appropriate Tools to Intercept and Obstruct Terrorism) of 2001
4. The 300+-page Patriot Act is devoted mainly to criminal procedure—surveillance and intelligence, law enforcement information sharing, search and seizure, detention, and interrogation.
5. Definition—material support includes:
    a. Currency or monetary instruments or financial securities
    b. Financial services
    c. Lodging
    d. Training
    e. Expert advice or assistance
    f. Providing safe houses
    g. False documentation or identification
    h. Communications equipment
    i. Facilities
    j. Weapons, lethal substances, explosives
    k. Personnel
    l. Transportation
    m. Other physical assets, except medicine or religious materials
6. Material support to individual terrorists
    a. *Actus reus*
        (1) Provide material support to individual terrorist
        (2) Conceal or disguise nature, location, source, or ownership of material support or resources
    b. *Mens rea*—intending or knowing support or resources are to be used in preparing or committing list of crimes helpful to terrorists

7. Material support to terrorist organizations
    a. *Actus reus*—provides material support or resources to terrorist organizations
    b. *Mens rea*—knowingly provides material support
8. Most-argued issues in material support cases are constitutional
    a. Due process—term "material support" is void for vagueness
    b. First Amendment—providing material support violates right to free speech and association

CHAPTER SUMMARY

To maintain themselves, governments everywhere have always had to rely on laws to protect them against foreign enemies and ensure the allegiance and loyalty of their citizens. During times of national emergency, we must try to strike the proper balance between security and freedom.

Treason is an ancient crime, and is the only crime defined in the U.S. Constitution. Article III, provides: "Treason against the United States, shall consist only in levying War against them, or, in adhering to their Enemies, giving them Aid and Comfort. No Person shall be convicted of Treason unless on the Testimony of two Witnesses to the same overt Act, or on Confession in open Court." The treason sections in the U.S. Code flesh out these terms.

It is a crime against the state not only to commit treason but also to encourage others to overthrow the government by violence. Advocating the violent overthrow of the government is called sedition.

Sabotage is the crime of destroying or damaging property with the intent of interfering with and hindering preparations for war and defense during national emergencies. Espionage is another term for spying for the enemy. It includes gathering and communicating information harmful to national security and defense to hostile groups or nations.

Some of the recent legislation on these topics is part of the USA Patriot Act. This is probably the best known of the recent acts. It is an acronym for "Uniting and Strengthening America by Providing Appropriate Tools Required to Intercept and Obstruct Terrorism." Aimed at terrorists, it was passed and signed into law on October 16, 2001, after the devastating September 11 attacks on the World Trade Center and the Pentagon. The new laws divide terrorism into two kinds—international and domestic. Domestic terrorism involves acts within the U.S. Acts outside the U.S. are deemed international terrorism.

A number of sections of the U.S. Code are available for prosecuting crimes related to terrorists and terrorist organizations. Among the crimes specifically aimed at terrorism are U.S. Code Title 18, Chapter 113B, "Terrorism", the Anti-Terrorism and Effective Death Penalty Act (AEDPA) (1996), and the USA Patriot Act (2001).

Among the offenses in these new laws are: 1. use of certain weapons of mass destruction; 2. harboring or concealing terrorists; 3. providing material support to terrorists; and 4. providing material support or resources to designated foreign terrorist organizations. The fourth-listed law has probably been the one most utilized by the government.

A number of legal challenges have been launched against these laws. The two most utilized challenges are due process (void-for vagueness) and First Amendment freedom of speech and association.

PRACTICE TEST BANK

Multiple Choice

1. In response to the terrorist attacks of Sept. 11, 2001, Congress passed the _____.
   a. AEDPA.
   b. RICO Act
   c. Act to Prevent Terrorist Attacks
   d. U.S.A. Patriot Act

2. The crime of espionage involves _____.
   a. sabotage
   b. obstructing the war effort
   c. spying
   d. aiding or giving comfort to enemies of the government

3. Many anti-terrorism laws are included in the 1996 _____.
   a. International Terrorists Act
   b. U.S.A. Patriot Act
   c. Anti-terrorism and Effective Death Penalty Act
   d. Act for the Prevention of Terrorist Acts against the U.S.

4. The crime of _____ involves encouraging others to overthrow the government by violence.
   a. conduction
   b. sedition
   c. espionage
   d. treason

5. According to the U.S. Supreme Court in the Cramer case, ____ saboteurs is not treason.
   a. mere association with
   b. corresponding with
   c. aiding and abetting
   d. discussing politics

6. The crime of _____ involves damaging or destroying property to hinder preparation for war or national defense.
   a. treason
   b. espionage
   c. sedition
   d. sabotage

7. Title 18 U.S. Code sections 2339A and 2339B of Title 18, U.S. Code make it a crime to provide _____ to terrorist organizations or terrorists.
   a. aid and assistance
   b. cover and concealment
   c. material support
   d. aid and comfort

8. The AEDPA was passed partly in response to the 1996 bombing of the _____ in Oklahoma City, Oklahoma.
   a. federal building
   b. U.S. arsenal
   c. Post Office
   d. airport

9. The offense of ____is defined as levying war, adhering to enemies or giving aid or comfort to the enemies of a nation.
   a. terrorism
   b. sedition
   d. espionage
   d. treason

10. One of the most famous American treason cases involved Julius and Ethel _____ who were executed for treason.
   a. Cramer
   b. Hess
   c. Alexander
   d. Rosenberg

11. The offense of _____ is the only one defined in the U.S. Constitution.
   a. espionage
   b. treason
   c. sabotage
   d. sedition

12. Terrorist acts committed in the U.S. are referred to as _____ terrorism.
   a. homeland
   b. internal
   c. domestic
   d. secondary

13. The most infamous domestic terrorist of recent years was _____.
    a. Karl Cramer
    b. Bernhard Goetz
    c. Timothy McVeigh
    d. George Siemens

14. The U.S. Constitution provides that a conviction of treason must be based on ___.
    a. a written confession or admission by a foreign government
    b. corroboration by physical evidence or testimony of three witnesses
    c. confession in open court or the testimony of two witnesses to an overt act
    d. proof beyond a reasonable doubt of remuneration from an enemy nation

15. Seditious speeches are termed seditious _____.
    a. conspiracy
    b. slander
    c. speech
    d. libel

16. The purpose element of the crime of treason is _____.
    a. to betray the U.S.
    b. remuneration
    c. revenge
    d. obtaining perquisites from foreign nations

17. As in Dennis v. U.S., during the 1950's, the primary targets of federal sedition laws were the ____.
    a. Jehovah's Witnesses
    b. Nazis
    c. Communists
    d. Seventh Day Adventists

18. The two constitutional issues involved in the crime of providing material support to terrorists are ____.
    a. void for vagueness and First Amendment freedom of association
    b. *ex post facto* and bill of attainder
    c. Fifth and Eighth Amendment
    d. procedural and substantive due process

19. The crime of treason has _____ *mens rea* elements.
    a. two
    b. three
    c. four
    d. five

20. Weapons capable of killing numerous individuals by use of disease, poisons, and

radioactivity are called weapons of ____.

a. multiple homicide
b. mass murder
c. mass destruction
d. multiple murder

21. Destruction and damaging are among the possible _____ elements of sabotage.

a. *mens rea*
b. circumstance
c. *actus reus*
d. concurrence

22. Treason is a _____ crime.

a. strict liability
b. vicarious liability
c. specific intent
d. mandatory death penalty

23. The circumstance element of sabotage is _____.

a. during war or national emergency
b. while enemies are spying on the nation
c. while the defendant is a citizen of the U.S.
d. the information will aid the enemy in attacking the U.S.

24. Most of the U.S.A. Patriot Act deals with _____.

a. sentences for terrorists including expedited death penalty appeals
b. creating new crimes
c. punishing sedition
d. procedural matters such as surveillance, search and seizure, etc.

25. The *mens rea* of providing material support to terrorist organizations is doing so _____.

a. intentionally
b. knowingly
c. recklessly
d. negligently

26. The U.S. Code separates spying into two separate crimes, _____.

a. time of peace and time of war
b. committed by U.S. citizen or non-citizen
c. domestic or transnational
d. overt and covert

27. The U.S. Constitution _____.
    a. leaves Congress free to create new definitions of treason
    b. leaves the courts free to create new crimes of treason
    c. prohibits the death penalty for treason
    d. limits the definition of treason

28. The current U.S. Code definition of sedition is limited to _____.
    a. seditious libel
    b. conspiracies that advocate violence against the government
    c. acts during actual time of war
    d. acts that are intended to aid enemies of the U.S.

29. The first sedition act in the U.S. was controversial because it included speech that _____.
    a. might be protected by the First Amendment
    b. encouraged young men to avoid fighting the French
    c. criticized the War of 1812
    d. advocated immediate, violent overthrow of the government

30. The federal Smith Act and Dennis v. U.S. (1951) involved laws against _____.
    a. espionage
    b. spying
    c. treason
    d. sedition

True-False

1. The primary aim of the U.S.A. Patriot Act is to fight international terrorism.
    a. true
    b. false

2. Sedition is the only crime defined in the U.S. Constitution.
    a. true
    b. false

3. Espionage consists of inciting others to violently overthrow the government.
    a. true
    b. false

4. Treason is an ancient crime.
    a. true
    b. false

5. Espionage means destroying government property.
    a. true
    b. false

6. Advocating the violent overthrow of the government is called treason.
   a. true
   b. false

7. Under U.S. law, espionage is only a crime during wartime.
   a. true
   b. false

8. In the U.S., treason can be punishable by death.
   a. true
   b. false

9. Under the U.S. Code, seditious conspiracy can be punishable by death.
   a. true
   b. false

10. The U.S.A. Patriot Act provides that it is a crime to conspire or attempt to provide material support to terrorist organizations or terrorists.
   a. true
   b. false

11. Sedition is a strict liability crime.
   a. true
   b. false

12. The U.S. Constitution specifies the type of proof required to convict of treason.
   a. true
   b. false

13. The right of peaceful association is protected by the Fourth Amendment.
   a. true
   b. false

14. The most commonly prosecuted crime against the U.S. since Sept. 11, 2001, is providing harboring or concealing terrorists.
   a. true
   b. false

15. Timothy McVeigh was a domestic terrorist.
   a. true
   b. false

16. Julius and Ethel Rosenberg were executed for allegedly passing American atomic secrets to the Russians.
   a. true
   b. false

17. According to the U.S. Constitution, one of the ways treason may be proved is by confession in open court.
    a. true
    b. false

18. According to the U.S. Constitution one of the ways treason may be proven is by the testimony of at least three witnesses to the same overt act.
    a. true
    b. false

19. The first U.S. sedition law was passed in 1917.
    a. true
    b. false

20. The first U.S. sedition law was limited to active advocacy of violent overthrow of the government.
    a. true
    b. false

21. In the 1700's Britain had no laws against treason.
    a. true
    b. false

22. Murdering the President of the U.S. would be an act of sabotage.
    a. true
    b. false

23. The crime of espionage involves information.
    a. true
    b. false

24. Sabotage is a strict liability crime.
    a. true
    b. false

25. Espionage during time of war is a vicarious liability crime.
    a. true
    b. false

Fill in the blank

1. _____________ is the more common term for espionage.

2. _____________ is advocating the violent overthrow of the government.

3. The U.S. Code prohibits providing ___________ support to terrorists or terrorist organizations.

4. Destroying or damaging government property to interfere with national defense is called ___________.

5. Making war or aiding those who make war on one's own country is called __________.

6. The U.S.A. ___________ Act was passed quickly after the terrorist attacks of Sept. 11, 2001.

7. ___________ to the enemy means breaking allegiance to your own country and supporting an enemy country.

8. Julius and Ethel Rosenberg were executed for passing atomic secrets to the ___________.

9. Under recent legislation, implements of biological, chemical or nuclear warfare are termed weapons of ______________________.

10. Under section 2339 of the U.S. Code, it is a crime to ___________ or conceal terrorists.

11. The *mens rea* of providing material support to terrorist organizations is ___________.

12. Damaging or destroying is the *actus reus* of the crime of ___________.

13. Seditious writings are called seditious ___________.

14. Laws prohibiting providing support for terrorist organizations may run afoul of the ___________ Amendment's freedom of association.

15. The ______________________ doctrine may invalidate some anti-terrorism laws.

<u>Essay</u>

1. Compare and contrast sabotage and espionage. Be sure to provide examples.

2. Discuss, define, compare and contrast treason and sedition. Be sure to provide examples.

3. What does the U.S. Constitution say about the crime of treason? Be sure to provide examples.

4. What are the two main Congressional Acts that deal with both domestic and international terrorism? Discuss some the things that are crimes under each.

5. Compare and contrast domestic and international terrorism. Be sure to provide examples.

CHAPTER 13 ANSWER KEY

Multiple Choice

1—d (463)	2—c (480)	3—c (481)	4—b (468)	5—a (466)
6—d (478)	7—c (484)	8—a (484)	9—d (464)	10—d (466)
11—b (463)	12—c (482)	13—c (484)	14—c (464)	15—c (468)
16—a (466)	17—c (469	18—a (486)	19—a (466)	20—c (483)
21—c (480)	22—c (466)	23—a (480)	24—d (484)	25—b (485)
26—a (480)	27—d (465)	28—b (468)	29—a (468)	30—d (468)

True-False

1—T (463)	2—F (463)	3—F (480)	4—T (464)	5—F (480)
6—F (468)	7—F (480)	8—T (464)	9—F (468)	10—T (484)
11—F (468)	12—T (464)	13—F (486)	14—F (484)	15—T (484)
16—T (416)	17—T (465)	18—F (465)	19—T (468)	20—F (468)
21—F (465)	22—F (479)	23—T (480)	24—F (480)	25—F (481)

Fill in the blank

1—spying (480)	2—Sedition (488)	3—material (484)	4—sabotage (489)
5—treason (464)	6—Patriot (463)	7—Adhering (465)	8—Russians (466)
9—mass destruction (483)	10—harbor (483)	11—knowing (485)	12—sabotage (480)
13—libel (468)	14—First (486)	15—void-for-vagueness (486)	